YOU CAN'T SELL RIGHT FIELD

A *Cape Cod* NOVEL

YOU CAN'T
SELL
RIGHT FIELD

BRIAN TARCY

You Can't Sell Right Field

This book was designed by THE FRONTISPIECE. The text face is Mercury Text G1, designed by Jonathan Hoefler, with other elements set in Trade Gothic Bold Condensed No. 20 and Aldrich.

To the townies who live and work on Cape Cod,
or in any resort community.

TABLE OF CONTENTS

1 *Bobby Has Money*

2 *Vermouth*

3 *Different Sides Of The Bench*

4 *Pool Party*

5 *Fireworks*

6 *Friday Tour Guide*

7 *Summer Day At Mission Pond*

8 *Losing Streak*

9 *Balloons*

10 *The Moon & Stars Strategy*

11 *Red Cranial Woodpecker*

12 *Dreamer's Row*

13 *Free Tickets To A Train Wreck*

14 *Market Revolution*

15 *Meeting On The Pitcher's Mound*

16 *Tastes Like Chicken*

17 *Divided We Stand*

18 *I Hate My Brain!*

19 *Bobby's Flyer*

20 *Banks Love Shysters*

21 *Extra Innings*

22 *Freedom of Speech*

23 *Pompous Circumstance*

1

BOBBY HAS MONEY

Out of left field, Bobby Linster sold right field. You can't sell right field. But I didn't realize it. I don't know how I missed the point that my best friend actually sold our right field, but I simply drank his beer and celebrated his good fortune and ignored the fact lying right there on the table in front of us. Bobby bought six rounds in a row. It was unprecedented.

The next morning, as I returned from a piss and lowered my dehydrated body back into bed with Lisa Burton, I repeated the story from the previous night.

"Do you realize what this means?" she said.

"It means Bobby's loaded."

"Bobby's not loaded. You call the little that he got *money?* It just means someone spent a lot of money for part of our ball field. Why would anyone do that?"

Lisa is so smart. She, like me, is 40. She is my girlfriend and I like her a lot. I smiled and, of course, said nothing even though I really did think it meant that Bobby was loaded.

Every game, Ed Zems taped the same list to the bench.

BATTING ORDER
Corey Everest, P
Cindy Morris, C
Charlie Alderdi, 1B
Bobby Linster, 2B
Cletis Bord, SS
James Gould, 3B
Alex August, LF
Gerald Zerck, CF
Lisa Burton, RF
Dawn Williams, SF

The first time I should have thought about what this all meant was the night before, the last day of June. We were in the Wild Bird celebrating. We had won that evening, 17-14 on a 6-run rally in the last inning. By the time we had figured something was up, there were only four of us left in the Bird – Bobby, Alex, Charlie and me. Everybody else had gone home because they had one to go to. Not us. I would eventually go to Lisa's. But it was not my home, even though with her I felt at home.

Bobby kept insisting on buying rounds from Jane, the bartender, and he had a big stupid grin on his face when he did. Same stupid grin he had earlier, after hitting the game winning triple. Then, he caught his breath and smiled big, a giggling-underneath smile, laughing about money we were all sure he didn't have.

At the bar, we could tell something was up, and tequila fueled our investigation. Alex insisted that something was indeed up before Charlie or I even noticed Bobby's uncharacteristic tavern generosity.

"Bobby's at the bar buying us all a round again," Alex said to me. Alex, who I've known since we were 8, is a lawyer.

"Something's up, Cletis. I'm telling you, something's up."

My name is Cletis Bord. I play shortstop.

It was uncharacteristic of any of us to buy two rounds in a row—a sure indication that a winning lottery ticket lurked nearby. It turned out, indeed, to be some such thing.

"Whipping Post" was on the jukebox. What a thing to remember. *Sometimes I feel like I've been tied...*

Charlie, as he could, insisted an answer out of Bobby and when we first found out that he sold his family's land that sliced through right field we were ecstatic for him. Alex especially. Bobby was now our friend with money.

After splitting $1 million with his five brothers and deducting taxes, he had $89,000. Can you imagine?

I am Bobby's best friend, and the garbage man in his neighborhood. For Bobby, who all these years later still worked the night shift at the Ocean Market, the money was a good reason to buy some drinks for his friends. He felt rich beyond belief. Pinch him. His life had changed.

Things around here have always been changing. Things have always been the same too. It's like that in Vermouth, on Cape Cod, where we live, where we grew up, where our lives have somehow mixed together for almost four decades. But for us, the connection is still about baseball. Why? It has always been about baseball or, now, softball. That's how it is. We are still together. We remain a team. The town team. The Townies.

As the shortstop I've got a quick glove, nimble feet and an arm to throw from deep in the hole. I have redefined the idea of a garbage arm. Mine is toned from tossing thousands of garbage cans a week.

Don't be jealous of this garbage gig of mine. Sure, the money isn't good and the smell made me throw up every day for two years until I finally was able to ignore it. But it really isn't as good as it sounds. As Bobby always says to me, women aren't nearly as impressed with the garbage man gig as I think they are. Funny guy, that Bobby.

I discovered that my childhood dreams from long ago melted into this daily reality of survival. Garbage in, garbage out—everybody's got a mantra. When I was young, I dreamt of traveling the world and putting up skyscrapers. I still had the same daydreams, even as I travel the town and pick up trash.

We're good, the Townies, that is. Ten of us are regulars, including the eight who grew up here. The eight of us played Little League together, graduated within three years of each other. We've celebrated marriages and children while living through divorces, and the deaths of our parents. Even though my parents are still alive and only live four miles away from me, we haven't spoken in more than a decade.

The night Bobby told us about the land sale, we played Gorman's Landscaping. Gorman's was in first place before the game started. We were in second. Gorman's had not lost at all and we had lost only once, to Vermouth Concrete. I'm convinced we only lost that game, because our best player, center fielder Gerald Zerck, was missing with a bad case of Anheuser-Busch flu. Another daylong hangover for Gerald Zerck cost us another game. He was, we laughed to ourselves, our temperamental star, yet we also agreed that he was worth the hassle. The catcher, Zerck's girlfriend Cindy Morris, was put in charge of getting him to the game, and that wasn't fair. No one cared about fair. Yet sometimes Cindy failed, and that, most of us agreed, was excusable and inevitable.

Brian Tarcy

In the first inning, Gorman's scored four quick runs as we played like the Bad News Bears—Bad News Townies—making dumb errors that compounded as we started bitching at each other with each subsequent brain-dead decision in the field. Throwing to the wrong bases. Two infielders and an outfielder all yelling, "I got it!" at the same time only to watch as the ball fell between them. It was funny. The other team was laughing.

In the second inning, Gorman's scored another four runs but this time they were simply hitting it where we weren't. This is always a good baseball strategy, one that I try to employ every time I bat—hit'em where they ain't. And it's also not a bad life strategy that's employed, I'm sure, by garbage men of every kind, everywhere.

In truth, our strategy those first two innings was the opposite of my stated one. We hit it right at the other team. Lazy ground balls to second. High loping fly balls to center. I hit a line drive directly at the first baseman. Zerck was robbed of a home run. And after two innings, Gorman's was scorching us 8-0 while their square-headed pitcher inexplicably had a no-hitter going.

Ed Zems screamed at us. He was the guy in the Hawaiian shirt—our so-called manager. Ed once played major league baseball for the New York Mets. A backup first baseman for a half a season, Zems played behind a monster-sized All Star who hit 27 home runs in 143 games. Zems, who carries his own baseball card everywhere he goes, essentially had a cup of coffee in the big leagues. It is more than any of us have had, as he is quick to remind us.

Now, he screamed and stomped, crazy rants—causing some on the team to point fingers and rant along in rhythm. The Zems' style was intimidation and teasing, a mixture of all the worst possible qualities of any schoolyard chum you could think of. I saw it as only baseball and could laugh off his behavior. Others were a bit more disturbed about him, but when we started winning it didn't matter. In Vermouth softball, winning is everything.

Zems moved to Vermouth 12 years ago and became our manager a year later in the Wild Bird. That night, he was flashing his baseball card around trying to pick up Alex's wife at the time, who soon became Alex's ex-wife, and shortly afterwards became Zems' ex-girlfriend. Alex is our left fielder.

How does a guy who is trying to pick up your left fielder's wife become the manager of your softball team? He had his own baseball card.

Of course, nothing is that simple, but it is how Alex explains it. On the bench at the first game Zems coached, Alex actually had this conversation with Zems.

Alex: What the hell is wrong with you?

Zems: If you raise your hands up above your shoulders, you'll have a more level swing and hit more line drives.

<hr>

In the third inning, Alex led off with a line drive double in the gap between the left and center fielders. Zerck was up next and after watching two high pitches he sliced a hard bouncer past the shortstop and suddenly we had runners at first and third with no outs.

"I never understand why we bat the girls back to back," Charlie said to me. "Lisa then Dawn. Just when we've got something going."

Charlie could be such a stupid bastard. In fact, Lisa had more hits than he did, and Dawn was on base at least as much as he'd been recently. Some things, I've learned, are better left unsaid. And arguing with stupid people is just plain dumb. Arguing with Charlie is dumber. So I said nothing, at least not out loud.

And the next thing I knew Charlie was cheering with the rest of us as Lisa, with a perfect inside-out swing, put a soft popup over the second baseman's head. 8-1. Lisa Burton!

No outs still. But Dawn grounded to third base for a third-to-first double play. The throw across the field beat Dawn by a step. So, Zerck stood at second as Corey Everest, our pitcher, came to the plate. Corey, who owns the Wild Bird, and therefore is the key to our after-game activities, flew out to center in the first inning. It was a long fly. In this at-bat, he whacked it even farther. And the center fielder loped underneath it for a can-of-corn catch.

As we ran on the field, Zerck smacked his glove and said to me, "I hope you weren't paying attention to how that rally died."

"Attention to what?" I said. It's our running joke. He claims I never pay attention to anything.

"For once, that's good," he said. "Cause we're still gonna win. You know." And he ran to center field.

I knew.

Two innings later, we were down 12-3 and the stupid infighting began again. Charlie, of course, was the main instigator, yelling at us for any little mistake. After I threw to the wrong base, he was livid, walking halfway across the infield at me before turning back to first base. I think he saw that I was more pissed.

In the sixth inning we rallied for eight runs as, like a miracle, our hits discovered the wonder of vision. Seeing-eye hit after seeing-eye hit. Bobby high-fived Charlie after Charlie hit a monstrous home run. I found that beautiful feeling in the middle of a game when things are going your way. Not many things compare to it. It's almost as if all of the world washes away, and you can only focus on the joy, speed, hustle, dexterity, coordination, and timing of the ball, bats, and gloves. These are specific things amounting to a lot more than that. When things go your way due to your total effort, yes, that is the essence of good softball. Or even when you get a lucky hit.

My hit was a popup dropped by the third baseman.

For the sixth through the eighth innings, we batted and went to the field, failing on offense and succeeding on defense. The only odd thing about those three innings was how Bobby kept saying he would give $100 to anyone who hit a home run. One hundred dollars! Bobby Linster!

"You're so full of shit," said Alex.

"No, really," said Bobby. It sure was weird.

"Where are you going to get $100?"

"Just hit a home run," said Bobby.

In the ninth inning, after we tied the game, Bobby hit his bases-clearing triple to give us a 17-14 lead. While standing on third base, he took a $100 bill from his pocket, waved it at the bench, and said, "Somebody's got to be a hero."

"Shit," laughed Zerck. "You should have told me you were serious."

After I popped out to third to finish us off in the top of the ninth, Gorman's Landscaping ended the game on three quick ground balls. Two were to me, including the final out of the game – and we were on our way to the Wild Bird. First, we shook hands across home plate, and then our team wandered to our bench where Charlie passed around a couple of fat joints that were shared by five of us, including Zems. The six who didn't smoke were, as usual, James Gould, Zerck, Corey, Dawn, Lisa, and Alex. Cindy, who was a selectman and thus, as we called her, a town father, did smoke God's gift but she didn't drink alcohol.

I reached in the cooler and grabbed a Budweiser. Somebody played some Bob Marley in their car speakers. The sun was up, and friends, old friends, surrounded me. Teammates. All of our lives we'd been coming to this baseball field and it was still the most amazing beautiful place to me. It was where I grew up—where I am still trying to grow up.

Brian Tarcy

Now, for us, it is a softball field instead of a baseball field. Same sport, different speed—like all of us. This field was beautiful in the unique way that only a field that you played on as a child can be. Like a member of your family, or that friend you've known forever.

You could actually see the ocean out past left field, over the marshy fields of bamboo, beach grass, bright yellow flowers, and poison ivy. I know it was too far, but I imagined seeing shorebirds at the coast. Out past right field, there were woods, thick musky woods, where deer sometimes dashed and squirrels certainly scouted. You could smell honeysuckle. I heard various bird songs. And when I wanted to, it seemed like I could still hear decades old laughter echoing around Mission Pond, which is down a path out of right field a half mile into the woods. I turned and stared out over the patch of left field green towards the ocean and realized, again, that I always have these goofy nostalgic thoughts after the games. And then someone nudged my arm and said, "Here, Cletis."

"These guys in suits came to my door about six months ago," said Bobby. "I just showed them away. But a month later, I got a call from my brother Matthew."

"Matthew?" I was surprised. He hadn't talked to his brother in about three years, ever since he borrowed money from Matthew, who sells used cars in Boston, and was then unable to pay him back. Circumstances changed, that was what Bobby said. Shortly afterward, Matthew drove here from Boston and walked in the Wild Bird after a game, found Bobby and called him "a piece of shit trash" in front of all of us. Then he chugged his scotch and walked out with his nose in the air.

That night, as we all stayed to console Bobby, about four or five rounds into the conversation, Charlie started in on how, maybe,

Matthew had a right to be upset, and how he hates it when Bobby owes him money. Then, Alex said Bobby owed him money too. Truth was, Bobby also owed me money. But I kept my mouth shut. Hell, I owed four credit card companies a lot of money. But Bobby was upset enough by the rounds of accusations that he never talked about his family again, other than telling me on Matthew's 50th birthday that he hadn't heard from Matthew in three years. That was the month before.

When we were younger, we knew everything about each other's families – far more than our parents would have liked, had we been dumb enough to tell them. Of course, back then we were full of trust— still new at trying on life.

"Yeah, I couldn't believe he called," said Bobby.

"What'd he say?" asked Charlie.

"He said he knew of a way that I could pay him back the money I owed him." Bobby smiled and quit talking for a brief beat. He spit out a muffled one-syllable laugh. "And I was surprised. I didn't hang up."

"Hey man, money," said Charlie. "Money talks. Money talks."

"All it ever used to do was swear at me," said Bobby.

2

VERMOUTH

Why would anyone buy right field? It fell right in front of all of us as the days wore on. Bobby and his brothers, it turned out, were the final piece in a 19-piece puzzle that had been put together for almost a decade by a man named Peter Junkin and his platinum wife, Melissa.

They appeared in town as the realest of deals, wheeler-dealers with spiel and meal, free wheelers and frequent flyers. They also worked behind the scenes, enticing 14 of the 19 landowners by contacting them with people who were not Junkins. The Junkins knew that to some people, their charisma would grate. So they researched everyone, and scientifically figured out the approach necessary to get a sale. For those five landowners that did meet the Junkins, they noted the couple were well-dressed and charming and exuded a daring confidence that the deal was already done. After Bobby and his brothers signed over their 16-acre slice of marsh, woodland, and outfield, the

Junkins—through an article in the Vermouth *Messenger*—introduced themselves to the town: "Couple Brings Dreams To Vermouth." The sub-head was "Zoning Change Needed."

All told, it turned out that the parcel put together by Peter and Melissa Junkin, along with various behind-the-scenes investors, was 327 acres. It was one whopping piece of land in this town where there was no other whopping piece of land to compare.

When right field is the final piece of one whopping piece of land that someone wants to develop, the answer of why to buy right field is clear as money.

"Why would he sell?" asked Lisa. "I mean, come on. This is where we live."

She had a point. It wasn't a point I thought of the previous night, as we helped Bobby spend his money, but now, in the calm of morning, as Lisa and I lay there talking, I started to register every conceivable and imaginary implication of this sale.

Mostly, I didn't want change.

Lisa Burton was in all of my homerooms in high school, as our last names were close enough alphabetically, in what was then a small high school, to anchor Bord to Burton. We'd known each other since we were eight, and we played on the same Little League team. Back then, she was the shortstop and I was the right fielder. In the three decades since, we attended each other's weddings, consoled each other through divorce, and finally slept together last year. We don't live together, but I sleep at her place a lot.

That happened about 18 years ago when our gang seemed to wander back to town at about the same time. I'd gone to college with a double major in fornication and inebriation, and returned with a degree in fun—though I could not produce the sheepskin. Lisa joined the army. Alex went to college, and Zerck wandered to California for five years. Only Bobby and Charlie stayed in Vermouth, and only Bobby worked at the same place as always, as the overnight butcher/

sandwich maker/stockboy/cashier/cleaner/security cop/night manager of the Ocean Market. He worked alone and has dealt for 20 years with the people of the night.

When Lisa returned to town she married a fun-loving carpenter who she met dancing at the Wild Bird while Zerck's band, Fish Story, played "Louie Louie." Lisa abandoned the carpenter six weeks after her child was born, and she always said that she did it because the carpenter had a gambling problem. No one knows the carpenter's side of the story since he left town shortly after that, and no one who I know has ever seen him again. Lisa's daughter, Emmy, is now 16, a lifeguard at the Market Beach, next to the Ocean Market.

I gently kissed Lisa's thick brown hair, and we snuggled closer as I put my college degree to use in my small town.

This is a boozy town, of course. Named after Vermouth, England, this fishing/tourist/growing community has more bars than churches by three times and more AA meetings than both put together times three. The list in the paper is funny. When we were teenagers, we said there was nothing to do. When we grew up, we discovered that there were plenty of places to do the one thing there was to do—drink. To be idle and rich here is as bad as being overworked and poor. It's all the same, only completely different.

"Another spectacular day," said Lisa.

"Yeah, God's up to some good stuff," I said.

"I'd like to know what the other people are up to."

"Who?"

"The people who bought right field."

It was July 1. We pulled into the parking lot at Market Beach at 9:30 in the morning and the lot was practically full. We parked in the back row, gathered up our beach chairs, our green cooler, and our towels, and headed to the stairs. As we sat down, about 20 feet from the flat ocean in a stirring sea of people that was dimpled with color-spun umbrellas, I asked Lisa, "What would anyone do with that little piece of land. I mean, it's in the middle of nowhere. Shit, it's always been that way."

"You're an idiot sometimes, you know that," she said, smiling. She laughed at me. "Think. Use that great big garbage brain of yours and give me an answer. Think about where you live."

Duh. Okay. What can I say? She was right, and I could figure it out in a second as soon as she told me to think about it because where I live and have grown up to most people is not a nostalgic, I-remember-when-I-was-8-years-old place. No, this is a place in New England where schemers come to get dollars.

I have no dollars to speak of but now Bobby had $89,000, free and clear, minus what he owed Matthew and what he paid for his friends to drink the night before. But Bobby was no schemer. Upon closer inspection, he might have been a schemee.

Land. Land is the essence of this place—land against ocean. This is the kind of place where people want to be.

Generations back my grandparents on one side relocated here from Kansas in the 1920s. My long-ago relatives that came here from Kansas were actually the offspring of two Bostonians who chased their fortune west during the Kansas land rush of 1893. Following this branch of the family tree, both sets of my Kansas great grandparents joined the land rush after Congress and President Grover Cleveland bought 6 million acres from the Cherokee nation for $8.5 million. They were among 100,000 who gathered in nine spots to claim land. And they ended up as neighbors. Then these great grandparents had children who ran in the fields together until they got old enough to roll in the hay. They had a nice Kansas wedding, and the very next day, they ran back to Massachusetts as fast as they could.

They landed in Vermouth.

Brian Tarcy

"Well, yeah, it's a pretty good place to others, I guess," I said.

"Yes it is. They come here on vacation," Lisa said, "and they spend money. Someone wants that land to get all that tourist money. Don't you get it? I'm worried, Cletis."

"I'm not," I said. "I mean it's nice but..."

I looked around.

I saw the sights of summer on Market Beach in Vermouth. Though way too crowded, these were still the sights of paradise to anyone who liked to visit the beach. Which is everyone I know. Most people like to see skin. And the ocean water feels good to the body and soul. Sandcastles and plastic shovels. Sounds of laughter. The smells of the salty fresh Atlantic. This is Vermouth. This is my hometown. Here, teenagers sneaked beers and kisses at the periphery while old folks in faded lawn chairs watched with disdain, or maybe envy. Moms gathered, as if a different species and chattered.

And, of course, license plates from places like Connecticut, New York and Ohio were scattered throughout the parking lot. This was a place where people came on vacation. There had to be a reason.

"Yeah, it's pretty nice," I said, quickly adding in, "I guess."

"Don't you ever travel?" she asked. "Have you ever been anywhere else? Other towns?"

"Not lately. But you know that I've been places."

She smiled.

"I don't even have to ask where. Let me just ask you this. Have you ever noticed that almost every other town in America looks the same? Same crappy chain restaurants. Same crappy box stores. Same highways connecting to huge malls. And the same population of folks disappointed with life."

"Well, on the first two, yeah," I said. "But most everywhere I've ever been, people to seem to like where they are. And they seem to like life well enough, same as here."

"It's different here," she said.

I smiled at her. "It's the same everywhere," I said, although I wasn't sure that was true.

3

DIFFERENT SIDES OF THE BENCH

"I think I see my boat," Alex shouted across the outfield to Zerck. At this point in the game, the temperature was a balmy 79 degrees and the sun sank slowly through the all-blue sky.

From the bench, Ed Zems yelled out, "Turn around and pay attention to the batter!" As he yelled, sunflower seeds shot from his mouth and Charlie started laughing. It was July 3, Monday night and we were beating Carson's Cars 8-2 in the sixth inning. On the next pitch, a fly ball that caused Alex to move only two steps to his left ended their half of the inning and we ran in to bat.

Early July in Vermouth is postcard season. Actually, any good photographer knows that the way sunlight reflects off the water along with everything else here is better in September, but that is of no concern to those only here in early July. To tourists, we live in a postcard. And they're right. Our colonial buildings and old stone churches have quintessential New England charm, while the coast offers Hallmark views of sailboats dancing.

"That was it wasn't it?" Alex said to Zerck as they jogged in. He was referring to his wooden schooner that had the name "Perfect Day," before it was taken by the IRS, and sold in an auction to a doctor who named it "Ann" for herself.

"Yeah, I think it was."

"Bastards," said Alex for the 900th time, "It's not fair, you know."

Zems pushed his way down the bench to his two outfielders. He grinned.

"Nothing is fair," he said. "Remember that. Nothing is fair!" He spit. "Except for baseball. So forget pathetic little problems and pay attention out there, damn it!"

This was Zems' usual kind of outburst, the type we'd seen from time to time. This time, though, he didn't go on and on. He stopped, tossed his lit cigarette to the ground and ground it down with the ball of his right foot. He was barefoot, as always and his shirt this night was green, white and orange. It stuck to his back in a big splotch of sweat. He plowed his way back to the other side of the bench, his big gut knocking into me for the second time in a minute.

"What's his problem?" Bobby asked.

"Who the hell knows," I said. "He wants to get down to the other side of bench, I guess."

Zerck was getting ready to bat, but Zems was now glaring at Gould.

"I think he's angry about that big thing in the paper today," said Corey Everest, looking over at Zems. "Ed wanted a part of it. The word is that Gould is in on it, but Ed is not."

I hadn't seen the paper although everybody was talking about it when I arrived for the game at 5:00. The Vermouth *Messenger* had a front-page feature story on Peter and Melissa Junkin, introducing them to the town and proclaiming their plan "a grand vision" that will transform the area. Usually, when anyone talked about news, it was

Brian Tarcy

Charlie bitching about the President or Corey praising the President or Alex in one of his lawyer/show-off moods analyzing why they were both wrong.

Anything more controversial than whether you liked Bruce Springsteen—the team was split, though Zems was a fan—would qualify as the kind of subject that would send half of us into our favorite non-important discussion—who would win a basketball game between Superman and Michael Jordan? I said Michael because there is no way Superman could guard him, but Bobby was convinced that Superman's superpowers would undoubtedly include a dead-eye jump shot from 60 feet.

So when people started flashing the *Messenger* around the bench before the game, Bobby and I were embroiled once again in all the implications of superheroes versus super humans. And Zems, in a sour mood, walked over. "Suppose," I asked, "the Fantastic Four plus Superman took on the Michael Jordan, LeBron James, Wilt Chamberlin, Larry Bird and Kobe Bryant?"

"All I know," said Zems, "is that if Jesus played hoop, they'd all lose."

"No arguing with that," I said.

Bobby nodded in agreement, "Yeah, with the miracles and all. Easy win, even one on five."

Zems smiled at that.

Meanwhile, Zerck stood in the batter's box.

Gould walked by us to get water from the cooler, but Zems stuck his body in the way. Then he glared, again.

"What the hell is wrong with you," Gould shouted at Zems.

Zems huffed. He stared. He drew a breath.

"What? I'm not good enough to include in your scheme?"

"You had your chance. You had a million chances. You delivered nothing," said Gould. "You and your baseball card!"

Bobby, who had by this time backed away from the whole confrontation, nudged me. He looked at me as if to say, *Can you believe it?*

Well, the confrontation, yes, I could believe it. But the bigger picture was somewhat overwhelming. Everything was about to change, that much I figured out. Somehow James Gould was involved, which though not officially surprising, I guess, was still disappointing, if not sad. The fact that Zems tried to get involved was not at all surprising, so it wasn't sad or disappointing. Just expected.

Then Zems turned and walked away from Gould.

"Good luck," he said, his words landing like spit on the infield dirt.

Gould said in general to all of us watching, "When you guys see the plan, you're gonna love it."

Zerck hit an easy ground ball to the shortstop.

"It's gonna be great," said Gould.

Lisa followed with an equally weak grounder to the third baseman.

"It's gonna revolve around Mission Pond. The place of our childhood made famous!" said Gould with a smile.

Dawn singled to left.

"What about the baseball field?" asked Alex.

Corey's one-pitch at-bat produced a line drive at the second baseman. Three quick outs.

"This baseball field?" Gould pointed. "Oh, well, you know, I think we can save it. But you know, this is a prime spot here. This elevation, that view."

His words trailed off and then he just smiled out at the ocean, seeing something different, I think, than I saw.

In spite of ourselves, we won the game 8-4 and we gathered around the bench popping open beers and changing cleats. Zems gathered the bats into a bag. Gould walked over to help.

With various degrees of subtlety—Charlie had none, staring bluntly—we all watched and listened. We anticipated something, but nothing happened. Gould methodically gathered softballs into the white pickle bucket. Zems huffed around leaning down for bats, then individually placing them in the black Nike bat bag. No one on the bench talked, gazing into the dramatic void, forced to listen to Zems grunt and breathe.

"All done," said Gould once he'd finished.

"Thanks," said Zems.

The rancor was gone. Zems was focused, gathering and then carrying equipment to his black Cadillac while refusing even Charlie's offer of intoxicating smoke. Alex carried the bases to the Zems' car and popped them into the back corner of the trunk while I carried his cooler and threw it in after the bases.

"It's not over, you know," said Alex.

"I know," replied Zems.

Alex pulled off his hat and ran his hand through his long, stringy hair.

"Nothing happens without a zoning change, you know that," said Alex. "And that takes an election."

"Yeah I know," said Zems. "Issue one. Fat chance that loses. I don't care anyway."

I didn't either. Or did I? I wasn't as sure as I had been. It certainly wasn't the kind of thing I would have ever cared about before—let it happen or don't. Except this time when it started to happen, I would inevitably discover that I hated it. In fact, normally I would have let a big change to my town go forward without a thought, until I was forced to think about it because of its actual presence. But this time, I knew people involved, so I paid attention. Everybody had a stake, it seemed, and the alliances—people sliding to different sides of the bench—were taking shape as I watched.

These were my friends. It was all really weird.

I had a stake too. That was the thing. I lived here. I knew the lay of the land, especially my garbage route. I drove the roads same as everyone else—fighting the coffee fanatics beeping their way into Dunkin Donuts. I swam the ocean at Market Beach. I knew where the sandy path into the water was. I spent half of every summer lazing by Mission Pond, right on this land—the land Gould and his new friend Peter Junkin planned to develop. This was my town too, even though I didn't have money or land. This was my baseball field, the same way it belonged to anyone who ever played on it. As I thought all this stuff, I felt like a tough guy—that's for sure. I was ready to dig my heels in. Into what, I still wasn't sure.

Brian Tarcy

4

POOL PARTY

In the middle of swimming pool volleyball, right after I lost the serve, Gould, who was on my team, told me he might be able to get me a job working at the new development.

"Probably more money than you're making," he said with a smile.

"I doubt it," I said. "You couldn't even match the signing bonus."

It was our annual Fourth of July pool party at Zems' absurdly designed house. Zems combined four themes—castle, colonial, modern, and spaceship—and then added in a swimming pool as the centerpiece. That was the order placed with local Vermouth architect Elliot Burren, who designed the most absurd-looking house that anyone has ever seen. Each successive room in the house followed the pattern—castle, colonial, modern, spaceship—so that as you toured the house, your sense of time as well as style became dizzy. Zems loved it this way.

He gave directions like this, "The beer fridge is in Castle Room

#3 and the microwave is in Modern Room #2," forced to add, "Down the hall to the left."

He lives in East Vermouth on one side of the huge Mission piece of land. On the opposite side of that there is the old neighborhood, Sandy Hills.

Over here, it's a lot nicer, fancier, bigger—all those words meaning richer. Zems lives in the woods but he has three acres of land, part of which he turned into the best Wiffle Ball field I have ever seen with a 12-foot tall fence in left field that he painted to look like Fenway Park's green monster. And his pool, 25 meters long with a low and high diving board, is what he calls the jewel of his property. Personally, I love the moat.

The sun was spectacular but our volleyball team was outmatched in seriousness and the game was over in the next series of serves by the hyper-competitive Gerald Zerck. After the game, I floated on my back in the pool, enjoying the afternoon sunshine. Next to the house, two full-sized grills plus a tabletop gas hibachi were being played to perfection by Ed Zems and Cindy Morris. And on the stereo—the pool had underwater speakers—the Beach Boys sang of endless summers.

Gould swam over to me.

"Listen, Cletis," he said, "I'm serious about the job thing. This new development is going to be great, and I can help you."

There is no statement in the world that I am more skeptical of than when someone tells me they can help me. Yeah, they'll help me. They'll help themselves to whatever they want. Gould should have known better, and he probably did, but I think he felt compelled to somehow try to get my approval. It wasn't just me, of course. He'd been lobbying the whole party, some of whom, such as myself, were skeptical of a big development eating away our town.

"I don't want help," I said. "I'm a good garbage man."

"Don't you want to change, become better?"

"All right," I said, "I know how I'll become better."

"How?"

"Get me a cheeseburger, would you?"

With dual double-spatula proficiency the president of the Vermouth Chamber of Commerce and the chairman of the Board of Selectman controlled the grill. Smoke in a perfect plume floated over the swimming pool so that in the water I could smell cooked meat amidst the easy-to-breath Cape summer air.

Zems and Morris. They cook together every year, and every year it is the same kind of funny.

Ed and Cindy do not like each other. At all. So that's potential entertainment right there.

And now they danced again to the sounds of "Cheeseburger" "Hot dog!" and "Sausage!" On foil, by itself on the hibachi, bluefish smoked. There were two long card tables next to the grills where all the guests put their potluck items: Dawn's potato salad, Charlie's potato chips, Lisa's brownies, and Zems chicken wings. I brought a macaroni salad I learned to make from a New York Times magazine that someone had put in the garbage. On the far end of the card tables sat the keg of Heineken. One dog, Zems' collie named Rocky, roamed among the guests licking up scraps while two buzz-cut employees in blue EZ Chevrolet shirts hustled around picking up trash and wiping up tables.

On the Wiffle Ball field, Corey and Lisa organized the kids into two teams of six. All the kids played, even Lisa's daughter Emmy. Every other minute I could hear one of Charlie's three kids screaming "Safe!" or "You're crazy!" or something from their dictionary of overused expletives.

It was 1 p.m. Zems and Cindy had already attended their official stuffed-shirt town gatherings in the morning. This was different—a gathering of old friends. This particular pool party had been going on since the first year that Zems took over as manager, back when he was trying to impress us. He still is.

But the fun part now is that these two who never talk during baseball games and have been battling for a year over Zems' plan to expand one of his three businesses, EZ Chevrolet—he also owns EZ Furniture and Zems Liquors—must coordinate together as a perfect team. They produced not political crossfire, just juicy cheeseburgers and perfectly charred hot dogs for a gathering that was older than any dumb political battle. It was the team: spouses, friends, and various others. We thought of ourselves as the cool people of Vermouth. Actually, I thought of myself as lucky to get to hang out with the cool people of Vermouth.

In shifts, friendships gathered around the pool, sitting peacefully on white wrought iron chairs and eating at matching tables. Zems and Cindy worked the fires.

I climbed from the pool, dried off, and asked Zems for a cheeseburger.

"Great day, huh?" he said. As the small talk of a big holiday turned, I thought, to the weather.

It was indeed a great day, a classic Fourth with the shouts of kids floating in the air among the powerful aromas of sea breeze, grilled food and lots of coconut oil. A couple of pesky seagulls hovered nearby.

After I acknowledged the beauty of the day, Zems asked, "Can you believe it?"

"Yeah, really, I think it's a great, great day."

"No," he said.

"Great, great great?"

He put his spatula down and personally delivered my cheeseburger. Its flavors tickled the air, steam rising and cheese still visibly folding at the corners. Zems grabbed my arm, and literally pulled me aside.

"You know what I mean," he said in a slurred whisper. "Can you believe it?"

Brian Tarcy

"Gould?"

"Yeah! Look, Cletis, this is going to change everything."

"Yeah, but everything always changes anyway."

"You don't understand," said Zems. "We need in on this deal." His head shaking slightly, he tried mightily to look me in the eye. "You know Bobby better than anybody. Bobby knows these guys. Get me in. Get me back in. You and me. I'll teach you. Me and you," he said. "We can be part of it."

"Ed, you're funny," I said. He grabbed my arm. I pulled it away. "Another time, okay?" I laughed and walked away.

And a half-hour later I should have expected him to be passed out. But since I knew Zems well I was not at all surprised to see him dancing and shaking off sweat with his big, drunk wife, Christine to the Rolling Stones' "Start Me Up."

After lunch, the sun became crushing and the gathering broke into two specific parts. Kids on one side, and Vermouth politics on the other. The kids continued with their Wiffle Ball game but this time only Lisa was smart enough to again fight the sun and avoid the subject that, fueled by alcohol, began to bounce around the pool. I watched Lisa running and laughing and I wanted to keep watching but against all my greater instincts, I found myself paying more attention to what I h

"I heard that Peter Junkin is somehow related to Walt Disney," said Cindy.

"Yeah, I think he's a second cousin two generations back, but he has a ton of Disney stock," said Corey as he nursed a Coca-Cola.

"Can you imagine what that's worth?" Charlie said almost as fast as all of us could think it. Charlie was my oldest friend, if not my best. He lived next door to me in Sandy Hills and has always stated the obvious in a way that he thinks sounds profound.

Some things are complicated. I really hate the practice of rating friends. But Bobby, who is now my best friend, lived across the street from me. And Zerck, who lived three houses down from me, is my third best friend. Zerck was once my best friend and has fallen as low as 7. Obviously, for anyone who has fallen from 1 to 7, they might as well be off the list completely. But why rate?

Don't get me started on things I rate. Don't.

For instance, this development was going to be a ten out of ten in some direction. I just knew it. Somehow or other, it was going off the chart. Even I knew stuff about it. That's absurd. I try my best not to pay attention to anything.

"It's worth enough to turn this little tourist town into a real place on the map," said Corey, "a place that people will really *care* to come to."

But I didn't care about any double cousinhood away from Walt Disney. That didn't make Peter Junkin into anything more than a fast talker in my book. Of course, I'd never met the man.

Gould stood and walked around the corner of the pool to where Corey was talking to us.

"It's gonna be great for all of us," he said.

"Why?" asked Charlie. "What's gonna be there that's gonna be so great?"

"Everything," said Gould. And he really smiled big. "You want to hear?" he asked Charlie, a little too loud to be speaking to just Charlie.

"Yeah," said Zems, who turned to the conversation, "we'd like to hear."

Gould asked Zems for a writing board and a black magic marker.

"Really?" I asked.

"I have everything," said Zems. He pointed to stockiest of his blue shirt employees. The man walked to the house and returned momentarily.

Gould started talking. He started with a stutter, "Do you, do you..."

He sighed, took a breath.

"Look," he said and he stared right at Zems. "We all know that this place is special, and it offers all of us that live here an opportunity we wouldn't have anywhere else."

I thought he made a lot of sense. I turned to the Whiffle ball field and saw Lisa run from just the right angle. I smiled and filed that thought away.

"And we all remember when we were young, and Vermouth was great," he said.

Just then, into my brain out of nowhere popped thoughts about the two offers made earlier that day—a job offer from Gould and an even more intriguing opportunity from Zems. I didn't know really what he was talking about. But he was rich, so he must be smart about this stuff. It all made my head spin.

The blue shirt brought over a writing board.

"Do you agree that change is inevitable?" asked Gould, doing his best rendition of a preacher or a politician, "and if so, do you want to be involved in it now or do you want to be a bystander in the future?"

"Gibberish!" yelled Zems.

I was intrigued. Anything that bugged Zems so much had to have potential.

Zems' face reddened, as he walked away and started bouncing on the low diving board. He must have drunk nine beers and several scotches already, yet there he was, bouncing in perfect form on the diving board, arms down with the downward bounce. His Hawaiian shirt clung to his belly. All the while, he glared as Gould talked.

Gould ignored him and drew a big circle on the whiteboard. In it, he wrote "Vermouth Smart". And over those words, he drew a huge dollar sign.

"I've known all of you forever," said Gould, in a statement that felt sort of true, "and I'm offering you this opportunity because I feel loyalty to you." This added statement definitely smelled of snake oil disguised as coconut oil. I am such a cynic, but usually I'm right. Or at least I think I am.

"The smart people in this town will recognize the big change before it happens," Gould smiled.

He had short brown hair with a high forehead that shined. Outside the circle on the top right he put a big "B" and on the bottom right he put an "NY". And then he drew arrows from the B and the NY to the circle of "Vermouth Smart."

"The big change is inevitable because this is a desirable place for people who work in New York or Boston. They're coming. These big city people with their big city money want to come here and give a bunch of it to us."

This sounded great to me.

"They'll give as much as we want for a little piece of our town. And when they develop this little piece, along with the help of a bunch of us locals, they will transform Vermouth into something great. I'm telling you people..." Gould stood breathing hard, his hand drawing "$" on the board over and over. A droplet of sweat rolled down his shiny forehead towards his right eyebrow.

"I'm telling you. This is your opportunity."

And then we heard the thwang of the diving board. Zems spun a flip. We turned. He was in a cannon ball aimed to send a wave of water onto Gould. The water slapped the sign causing the darkened "$" to run into drippings of black ink. Someone nudged my arm.

"Here, Cletis."

Smiling, Gould said, "This is going to make Vermouth great again."

At 4 p.m., Cindy talked while Zerck gave drunken encouragement of her presentation on the environmental reasons why the development, which we learned was going to be called "Mission," would be disastrous. For one thing, any use of that land would use up way too much of the Cape's water.

Brian Tarcy

Water again. I'll tell you. This damn water stuff when you live in Vermouth—it's all you hear about. Water this and water that. I can't ignore it at all. So when Gould said, "Water's not a problem," I was happy as a cooked pie to hear it, even though I had no idea whether it was true. I was just happy to have someone tell me I could ignore it. I always like when that happens.

As for the project, Mission, I had no idea whether it was a good idea or not. I thought the name was stupid. It was not Mission Heights or Mission Commons or Mission Mall or Mission Place. Just Mission, after Mission Pond. I imagined this conversation.

"What are you doing tonight?" asked the boy.

"I'm going to Mission," replied the girl.

"Are you a Mormon?"

"No, I live in Vermouth."

Instead, I heard Cindy talk about water as if it were as valuable as money, beer, or cheeseburgers. It was the old rat-a-tat-tat of concerns about the single source aquifer—meaning all the water under the ground is connected, so pollute one part and you eventually pollute it all. I wanted to say, *Yeah, yeah yeah, the ice cubes in my drink are fine and tasty.* But I just listened. It wasn't my concern. I knew somebody would solve the problem.

"The way to solve the problem," said Cindy, "is to stop the building. This town has had enough. It can't take any more. Do you realize what a special place this is, what amazing species we have around here. Any more development, especially on that big parcel out by Mission Pond, is going to destroy not just the water, but everything. Terns, turtles, all sorts of God's creatures."

"But what about the jobs?" asked Gould. "Mission is going to create a number of jobs for people of the area."

"Working at a mall or a mini golf or a go-cart track is a job?" asked Zerck, incredulous. "C'mon man. You know this is a sham for your hotshot developer friends."

"Peter and Melissa."

"To make money. You know it. They or you don't care about the terns or the turtles," said Zerck. He paused, breathing audibly. "This is special land."

"And that's why it's so valuable," chimed in Zems as he literally walked into the conversation. "Special land holds special charms."

"There is one other thing," said Zerck. "Have you heard of the Red Cranial Woodpecker?"

"No," said Zems. He stopped walking.

Gould, who was sitting, leaned forward.

"Well, you know Victoria Manchester? She called me yesterday telling me about this bird, the Red Cranial Woodpecker, and how its only known nesting area north of South Carolina is by Mission Pond."

"The Red Cranium Woodpecker?" asked Gould.

"Cranial," said Zerck. "Red Cranial Woodpecker."

"Tastes like chicken," said Zems.

"Everything does," said Charlie.

"Except chicken," I said.

"Yeah, that always tasted like eggplant to me," said Zerck, smiling at Cindy.

"And eggplant tastes like Red Cranial Woodpecker to me," said Zems.

"Stop!" said Cindy, staring down Zerck. "This is serious. There may be no terns or turtles but that woodpecker is the real McCoy. This is an important bird that can stop Mission."

"What do you mean?" asked Charlie.

"Why is this woodpecker so important?" I asked.

"It's an endangered species."

"Not in South Carolina, right?" said Gould.

"The woodpecker is a sign," said Cindy. "A sign that everything in nature is running smoothly. If it's supposed to be here, it has to stay."

"How is that?" I asked. "If these birds in Vermouth are the only ones north of South Carolina, why are they a sign of anything other than a confused branch of the family tree?"

"Oh Cletis," said Cindy. "You have a lot to learn."

But I didn't want to have to learn.

5

FIREWORKS

"I feel like I've known you forever," said Lisa.

It was a line my ex-wife used right after she first met me and before our five years together that were nothing like bliss. I smiled at Lisa. This time it felt real, not a lie.

"You have known me forever," I said. My heart jumped little. I loved when Lisa talked to me like that.

It was getting dark when we wandered as a group on our joyful journey to Zems' Wiffle Ball field. These were my friends. I couldn't help but smile. In the distance in two different directions we heard firecrackers popping. At the front of this roundup of people Zems laughed full bellied, then Charlie did too.

Lisa and I held hands bouncing and walking. This was love. I was astonished. There was a sudden sureness of the moment. It was overwhelming to realize it. There I was walking with this crowd. And then there it was, I remember the moment like a photograph. In one magic step, I just fell into love with Lisa and I thought, well, that was simple. And I said it. Right there in private in front of everyone. No one heard but Lisa, but I said it.

"I love you."

I was in love with life, with everything about summer. I heard friends laughing, Charlie claiming he would hit a home run in each of the next three games, and Gould saying that if Charlie hits his three, he'll hit home runs in the next three games. This rolled like telephone tag through the group so that even Charlie's three kids and Dawn's husband the plumber were guaranteeing they would also hit home runs for three straight games. We were up to almost 70 home runs in a row when Zems yelled out, "Watch this!" and he lit his lighter.

In center field, set up by the blue shirts, were tubes, dozens of them. Zems bent and lit the first one and it shot off, whizzing for three or six seconds then finally exploding over the woods behind the center field fence in a glittering circle of yellow that blinked and streamed, finally turning into puffs of smoke which settled fast in the fading sunlight. I squeezed Lisa's hand. She smiled warmly at me, her brown eyes glowing with each explosion.

"Hey Cletis," she said.

I smiled at her with all my eyes.

"Did you think that was an error on me yesterday?"

She meant the play where she fielded the ball and threw it to Charlie who couldn't reach it. For one thing, she waited too long to get the ball. For another, she threw to the wrong base. And to complete the trifecta, her throw was way too high for Charlie to catch.

I shrugged my shoulders, not sure what to say, wishing she would say she loved me.

So I changed the subject and said, "Wow, look at that one," as blue and orange sparkles fell from the sky.

6

FRIDAY TOUR GUIDE

I was the teacher again, as I had been 14 times in the past four years—even during the end of my two-year nausea run.

"Just lift the can and turn it over the truck so that all the shit falls out," I said.

The fact that Vic cannot find me a qualified partner who will stay long term speaks volumes about something or other, but I am not sure that it doesn't just explain itself with the job title.

"It's cool to be a garbage man," I told Fred Glass, as I'd told all of his predecessors. "You're not going to believe how many times you get laid on this job."

And every single one of them believed me. Fred, ever hopeful, was no different.

Breakfast at 6:30 a.m. on Friday July 14 was the same breakfast of champions as always—powdered donuts and chocolate milk from the 7-11. It took me two years to figure out the proper recipe to be a garbage man. Two years of old-fashioned nausea as I tested Rice Krispies, bagels, toast, bacon and eggs, and pancakes before I finally settled on leaving ten minutes early in my old blue Chevy and buying junk food from the friendly heroin addict working the convenience store counter.

With Led Zeppelin as my primer and donuts as my fuel, I guided the Chevy past joggers down Main Street. I was glad the thing was running again. John, my mechanic who just replaced the water pump, told me it would soon need to be read its last rites. Ever since the Fourth of July, that's how it's been. One thing after another.

I drove while munching donut after donut and I could feel a strong brick forming in my stomach. Powdered sugar spilled onto my blue work pants as I headed off of Main Street onto Old Country Road towards West Vermouth. I turned the cap off of the chocolate milk and guzzled about half the bottle. A little dribbled down my chin, and, with perfect orchestration, I turned the corner into the expansive parking lot of T&G Services while wiping my chin with my shirtsleeve. I finished the turn, closed the milk bottle and stuffed two more donuts into my mouth.

After punching my time card, I sat in the hard, orange plastic chair, drinking rancid company coffee and checking out the morning *Messenger*. Once again, it was more Junkins. Today, there was a huge profile on the front page about the Junkins and their arrival in Vermouth. The paper quoted each of them extensively. I read enough of it to gather that Peter Junkin was a decorated fighter pilot and a former minor league hockey player. I turned the page and below two other stories about Mission I found an artist's rendering of a top view of the entire property. At the edge of our ball field sat the back alley of a mall. Over by thick woods around Mission Pond was drawn a minor league ball field with stands to hold 4,000 people.

I chugged the last half of my coffee and turned to the classifieds. I'd soon need a car. But as I began to scan for prices below two grand, Vic, the boss, introduced me to my new partner, Fred Glass, a paunchy young man of about 30 with a way too eager face. He was glad to meet me.

Any intelligent entrepreneur with a specialty in odor elimination would be able to sell a tourist's trip on my garbage route. It is not in good taste to describe the bad things I have seen and smelled here. I will simply say that the colors and textures combined with the odor make me think of what death looks like when it is having a party. This is because some people in this town are horrible slobs. They don't know how to cover or bag their garbage. I, and my stomach, have to deal with it. Pick a food, add some maggots, and I've seen it, smelled it and dealt with it.

But if you get past the smells, my route is a crazy nice tour of Vermouth real estate.

"These are spectacular houses," said Fred, who won't know of real spectacular until we wander to East Vermouth. Fridays the route goes through Vermouth Village, the center of town, and the outlying streets where half of the team lives.

East Vermouth, on Mondays, is a different animal all together. That's where Zems and Gould live, just on the outskirts of the 327-acre Mission Pond parcel. They live in a place called Palmer Hills, which is exclusive, gated, with big lots and homes for those of few scruples. Zems and Gould, both friends of mine, fit in well.

Gould once told me that, "Living up here, man, is like living where you always pictured yourself." He smiled at me. "You know," he said.

At the time, I was talking to him on his front yard just after emptying his barrels.

Brian Tarcy

In the race, I guess I lost. That is the message that I always found bouncing around inside the truck as I drove to the first house of the day. Although this was not East Vermouth, Fred was right. These were spectacular houses, unlike the studio apartment over Lou's Laundromat that I rented in South Vermouth.

Two streets into the route, after Fred's first bout of the dry heaves, I told him that he could drive and that I would hop in and out and get the trash cans.

Throwing trash cans is hard work, but on trips between streets or to dump off a full load it allows me to do the one thing of personal advancement that I can do as a garbage man. I read. In the front of my truck, I read more interesting books and magazines that people have disposed of than any CEO would ever have time to read. If you want to find the most educated man in your town, look in your garbage truck.

Unlike my neighborhood, these were homes, not just residences. They were old houses with giant two-winged grills set up on big farmers' porches. Out in the yards, American Flags flapped on poles next to giant oak or maple trees. Later in the day, young girls in flowing dresses would be sipping lemonade on the porch swing.

Lisa, on her inheritance and salary as a kindergarten teacher, lives out here with her daughter, Emmy. When we got to Lisa's street, I smiled. This street felt like a winner. I looked at her house, almost 100 years old and built about 8 feet from the street. I thought how it had been ten days since I told her I loved her. When I said it she smiled, I felt, sympathetically. So, picking up her trash felt mixed up, and part of me wanted to toss the garbage all over her yard and spell out, *Answer me!*

Alex lives out here too, somehow. His street is a couple down from Lisa, in a more questionable part of the neighborhood, still nice if you want. He takes on housemates from time to time, and sometimes they disappear without paying him rent.

Dawn and Cindy live on the same street. Dawn, who is vice president of Vermouth Bank & Trust, lives out here with her husband Jack Williams, a licensed plumber, and their 16-year-old son and 14-year-old daughter.

Cindy lives in the house that her ex-husband, Joe Morris the civil engineer, bought a couple years before she was elected selectman and they were divorced. Their three children, ages 10, 12, and 14, split time between the two. Joe, who is 17 years older than Cindy, lives in South Vermouth and remains one of her best friends.

Finally, in a long cul-de-sac near the end of the route lives Corey, in a large, ostentatious house that should really be located in East Vermouth.

As I toured the town, day after day after week after month, I noticed that all of these other houses were winners. They had the sweet garbage that turned the sourest. The homemade stuff that actually decayed, whereas in my neighborhood of cheap South Vermouth rentals, there were plenty of chemicals to keep our half-eaten pre-made packaged food looking almost as it did when the last bite was taken. Winning food was decaying food.

But my study of humans as a species of trash producers in this small town could only take me so far and I continued to discover daily, to my dismay and apparent surprise, the winners lived better than the losers did in every economic way possible. I never thought about these things until I had listened for years to the mindless ramblings of dumb-as-dirt partners or the repetition of bad songs on crappy radio while in my garbage truck. I had nothing to do, so I would look around and think, something I really hated to do.

Brian Tarcy

I started where I left off, in the office that morning, with the *Messenger*. By the time I had gathered a *Vanity Fair*, a *Newsweek*, three copies of *National Geographic*, an *Architectural Digest* and the previous day's *New York Times*, I had found a 10-year old Honda for $2,500 in the paper. I figured I could talk them down. Then I saw a story about new study showing that groundwater in South Vermouth was so polluted the entire area would need to have water piped in within two years, and even now drinking the water may cause cancer. In Vermouth, it seemed, you played Russian roulette with a water glass.

Later, when I drove, Fred looked at the paper and noticed a small article on page 3.

"This Red Cranial Woodpecker sure is a cool looking bird," he said. "Did you know they like Mission Pond because of the Hellfire Hawkweed, this weed that grows near blueberries. It says here it looks like a dandelion and Mission Pond is surrounded by them."

I knew exactly what he was talking about. I wanted him to shut up, but now that he'd mentioned it, I thought of the yellow flowers with the hairy leaves. They looked a bit like dandelions, only bigger. They were all over the pond at this time of year.

"For some reason," he continued, "these Red Cranial Woodpeckers have been drawn every year to Mission Pond and nowhere else. They only go to Mission Pond even though there is plenty of Hellfire Hawkweed and it's accompanying berry plants all over the coast from South Carolina to Massachusetts. No one knows why."

Fred showed me a drawing of the bird, with an all red head and a zebra-striped body. It looked really cool, I agreed, but I was sure I'd never seen one.

"But, you know, it tastes like chicken," I said.

"Really?" he asked.

I laughed.

7

SUMMER DAY AT MISSION POND

As my hand splashed through the water and grabbed at the blue carpet, I heard Alex say, "I dare you," to Zerck. Daring Gerald Zerck to do something is the same as forcing him.

"How much?" asked Zerck.

They were both sitting on the blue-carpeted raft.

"Man, I don't have to pay you for this. You're just chickenshit. As always."

"This will be easy," said Zerck.

"It would be easy for me. She'll slap you."

"I know her," said Zerck. "I met her at the Bird in May." He laughed at the absurd story. "Her name is Susan and she's like an accountant or something."

"It's Stephanie, she's a waitress and she likes lawyers," said Alex. "I'm positive."

"In your dreams."

"They're good dreams. Chicken shit."

Zerck laughed. One thing we all knew was that Zerck was no chicken shit. Insane? Yes. Stubborn and ignorant? Definitely. But chicken? No way. Not Zerck. This was the person who a couple decades ago walked into the Vermouth Police station smoking a joint. We cheered him on from afar.

Zerck, being Zerck, tried to make the case into a publicity stunt to fight marijuana laws but no reporters were interested. So he served his 30 days, anonymously, then went to journalism school. He was a reporter for a few years, until he realized that he could make more money cooking french fries at McDonalds, and switched to advertising. Along the way, he quit smoking dope. Instead, about a decade ago, he started drinking every day. Yet certain things about him remained steady—including his unsteadiness. At 40, he remained a great athlete who carried himself as if he were plugged into a 12-smokestack industrial power source while the rest of us ran on a couple AA batteries.

Zerck stood dutifully, like a man dared, dove off the blue carpeting and began swimming in his thrashing style towards the beach. There, on the other side of the beach from our homestead, sat a blonde in a yellow bikini on a white towel. She had arrived after we'd gotten in the water.

As Zerck swam, I heard a familiar shout of my name stretched through time. I turned to the woods at the side of the beach to see Lisa fly through the air with the greatest of smiles. She was, to me, a dream, in her green-and-white bathing suit with her hair in the wind and her arms flailing and waving. If I could have slowed down time this would have been one of my top moments to savor. Lisa Burton in the air. Laughing and smiling, smiling at me.

There she was with all of those curves that I had finally come to know. I watched as she fell through a background of blue sky and lush green trees into a great splash of Mission Pond brown water.

Cutting through a hill in the woods, along the right side of the town beach at Mission Pond is a dirt path on which to run with the thick rope swing. The swing and the path are designed to let you run and swing over the pond and release. At its highest you can swing 15 or more feet in the air over the water. About 25 yards past where the farthest rope swinger has ever landed is this big wooden float covered with coarse blue carpeting. I waited on this float for Lisa.

As Lisa splashed into the water, Charlie leaned from the path to get the rope as it swung back towards the land. He handed it to his oldest child, Mary, who is 14 and as full of herself as Charlie. The Alderdis behind her in line were Joey, 11, Sam, 10 and Charlie, 42. I like Charlie's kids, except for Sam. That kid is a punk.

The rope hung from an ancient, thick-limbed maple tree. As far as we could remember, it had always been there in one form or another. This current, 5-inch-thick, super sturdy version of the rope swing was installed by Zems' employees during his first summer with the team. Back then, he was always trying to impress us. I guess we're all just trying to impress someone.

As Zerck reached the beach, he walked to the blonde on the white towel and leaned down to her then suddenly jumped away. Alex pointed and laughed.

"What's he doing?" I asked.

"Trying to kiss her," laughed Alex, "and tell her he is related to Walt Disney."

"What? Why Walt Disney?" I didn't even bother to ask about trying to kiss her. That was just Zerck. This was the kind of thing that should get him in trouble with Cindy, if she found out, except that he's done stuff like this many times in front of her in the Wild Bird, and she always just laughs. Like we all do. But Disney?

"'Cause Zerck has decided that being related to Walt Disney is the way to the top in this town," replied Alex.

I knew the reference to the Junkin story.

"Zerck is insane," I said.

"He doesn't care. I dared him." said Alex.

"Yeah, I know."

Just then bits of the blonde-spewed venom were picked up by the wind and carried out to the float. "You are such a ... Do you know who ... You need to ... the hell is wrong with you! ... Grow up!"

Lisa laughed first. We all laughed.

"He's not chicken," I said.

Just then, Charlie and his kids began arriving on the raft and the balance went all off to one side. Alex, Lisa and I moved to the other side to give enough equilibrium to the raft to allow all incoming Alderdis onto the blue carpet.

Mary hoisted herself up first, immediately saying, "Gee, it sounds like Mr. Zerck went and made another mistake."

Then came Joey and Sam, side by side: Joey with longer hair and softer eyes, and Sam who already thinks of himself as the future Original Gangster of Vermouth. Of course, he has competition among his peers. When I see them around town, Sam and his friends on their bikes are wise-ass punks who don't give proper respect to their local garbage men. When Charlie climbed aboard, the once spacious float was filled to capacity.

"What was Zerck doing," asked Charlie. Now, Zerck was swimming back to us.

When Alex explained the basics, Charlie just shook his head.

He lightly punched Sam and said, "See, son, Mr. Zerck is one of my best friends, but don't be like him."

"Don't worry, Dad," said Mary. "Mr. Zerck is kind of a doofus."

"Hey," said Alex. "That's not nice."

"Yeah, but you're kind of a doofus too," she said. "You know, Daddy," she said, looking at Charlie, "most of your friends are doofusses."

"I know," said Charlie. Then he stood, grabbed his daughter under the back and legs, and flung her off the raft into the water.

Mary and Zerck arrived at the raft at the same time.

"Hey, Mr. Zerck," said Mary, hiding all her former contempt for Zerck under a strong aura of teenage flirtation. He smiled at Mary. He shook his hair. He looked at all of us on the raft, his lifelong friends in the place of our childhood.

"You are not going to believe this." He laughed, pulling himself onto the raft. Mary followed immediately.

He looked at Alex and laughed.

"*You are not Walt Disney! Do you know who that is?*"

We all did the same general shoulder shrug and head bob.

"That's Melissa Junkin."

Every one of us turned toward the beach and looked. It was a great, choreographed maneuver. Melissa Junkin, Walt Disney, this was almost the first place trophy win for the great Gerald Zerck.

"What'd she say?" asked Alex.

"We heard," said Lisa.

"We only heard part," I said. "What'd she say?"

"Well if we heard her, she can hear us," said Charlie. "Hey!" he yelled. He stood up, rocking the float. "Hey Melissa Junkin!"

"Hey Melissa Junkin!" yelled Sam, as if on cue.

"Well," Zerck laughed, "I tried to get her to just go along with the joke. You know, once I realized who it was. But she would have no part of it. She seems to think we are immature. I am immature."

"Wait. Haven't you met her? I thought you sold her an ad," I said. "Why didn't you stop when you realized who it was?"

"Alex dared me."

I looked at Alex. He grinned.

I turned back to the beach and saw the blonde in the yellow bikini stood up. She gathered her white towel and started walking away.

"Hey Melissa Junkin!" Charlie yelled again. "Hey Melissa Junkin!" All four Alderdis were chanting now. "Hey Melissa Junkin!"

She stopped. Then, very clearly, she gave us the finger.

Brian Tarcy

I came to Mission Pond often with my friends. But I came also for solitude. I had a silver raft that I inflated with my little red electronic air pump that I bought for my inflate-a-bed that broke after a year of heavy use. The pump still worked beautifully, making the three $49 payments that I made for the bed incredibly worthwhile.

To think of it, floating on the pond with six cold cans in the cup holders of my $26 silver Wal-Mart raft, I was more relaxed than I ever was on that $147 bed.

I have recalled, with beer theatrics more than once in the Wild Bird, that I took the bed from place to place for a year, six years ago when I was really down on my luck. I'd set my inflate-a-bed on the floor of Alex's garage for an entire summer. But that was long ago, before I found my steady garbage gig and an apartment over Lou's Laundromat.

I had a real bed now, but I still liked the raft in the sunshine on Mission Pond. It's quiet, even when it isn't because when I lay on the raft, if I want, I am able to hear nothing. On Mission Pond when the sky is blue, it's really blue. The clouds puff into a spectacular white. In the summer, everything is green except for the yellow flowers.

My friends were indulgent of my long drifts off into the pond. I slept, I dreamt. I thought. I didn't think. If I wanted I found a kind of silent communion with something greater than myself. Most religions brag about stuff like that. I remained glad that most religions force their flocks to places other than my silver raft on Mission Pond.

After I returned from floating, I sat on my yellow towel and grabbed a tuna sandwich from my green cooler. Except for two houses straight across from us, the pond looked the same as it did when we were eight. One of the houses, put up when we were in high school, sits up on a denuded, nitrogen-injected, green hill as a sort of top to the trophy. The other house, built a decade later under at least some conservation laws, was nestled in the woods. If a house were to be built today, conservation laws would be even stricter. Most likely, any owner building now would be, as all those who now build in Vermouth's finest areas, a braggart with lumber.

I chewed a bite from my sandwich, a little soggy from the ice in the cooler but perfectly fine otherwise. For a while, no one said anything. Lisa read *Sports Illustrated* while Charlie paged through *Popular Mechanics* and Alex listened to headphones. Charlie's boys were taking turns on the rope swing, while Mary was diving off the raft with two other girls her age.

Charlie laughed at Joey for landing close enough to Sam to send a wave over his head. It was his *ya! ya! ya!* laugh. I had heard it at this pond forever—that rope swing and this pond were the toys of our endless summertime. Except now, the endless part was coming to an end.

Charlie turned to Zerck, who was lying down comfortably, "I still don't get it, Ger. You sold her an ad, yet you went and goofed on her. I mean, I don't get it."

"I didn't recognize her at first and she didn't recognize me," said Zerck, sitting up.

I joined the conversation. "How is that possible?"

"I don't know, but I bet we both meet a lot of people."

"Yeah, but you spent hours with the Junkins, just three weeks ago."

"What can I say?" said Zerck. "I'm not good with names or faces."

"You mean you don't pay attention?" I asked.

Zerck gave me a wry grin.

"I guess she isn't good with names or faces either," said Alex, standing as he spoke. "I'm going swimming," he said.

"I think she knew who I was, or at least I think I know when she figured it out," said Zerck. "Right before I figured it out. And by that time, you know..."

"She wanted no kisses," laughed Alex, who stood firmly. He made no move toward the water.

"That didn't even bother her that much," said Zerck. "She just said, 'No thank you. Not right now.' "

"Not right now?" Alex asked.

"That was weird enough," said Zerck, "but when I said I was related to Walt Disney she got really mad. It was like she thought I was making fun of her, or something. That's when I figured out who she was."

"You kind of were making fun of her, weren't you?" I asked.

"Why would it matter? Making fun of Walt Disney?" asked Charlie.

"Don't you know anything?" asked Alex. "Peter Junkin is the great nephew or something of Walt Disney. That's where the money for Mission is coming from."

"That and banks," I said, acting like I knew where money comes from.

"And so the Mouse is coming to take over our town," said Lisa, "and there's nothing we can do."

"Nothing," I repeated.

"We could try to stop the zoning change in the election," suggested Alex.

"No one's going to care what we say," I said. "We don't matter. What power do we have?"

"You're right, no one's cares what we say," said Zerck with authority.

"That settles it then," said Alex. He turned and walked with a carefree bounce to the woods and grabbed the rope swing.

8

LOSING STREAK

Twenty-three softballs plus the white pickle bucket that held them went flying. One of the older softballs with loose stitching hit Sam Alderdi, who collapsed to the ground only to come up about 10 seconds later, silent and wiping away a baby-sized tear.

Twenty-three softballs and a bucket. Zems again. He actually brought his Scotch bottle to the game, which didn't help his already jumpy temper. His trigger had been getting faster the past couple weeks as the Mission project heated up. Now he screamed at Bobby who had just let a ball roll right through his legs. Zems was right. I mean, I felt like screaming too, but it was Zems who was hyperventilating like a maniac because he wouldn't stop.

We had already lost two games in a row, and we were losing again. It was July when the season was supposed to be in its glorious, summertime peak. Suddenly, the team found a way into a bickering losing streak. I wanted to make the bickering stop, but I didn't know how. Zems bounded up, looked at Bobby and then reached down and grabbed the white bucket. After tossing the bucket, he turned and waved his arms.

"Jesus H. Christ, Linster, what the Goddamn hell is wrong with your lazy ass! Is it too much to ask you to lean over for the goddamn ball! Is it too much to ask you to work a little for your goddamn team! Is it too much to ask you to, oh!" and he just stopped.

Both teams stopped to watch the outburst. I always imagined he learned these screaming techniques from the major leagues and was just paying it forward. More likely, as most of us learn our bad habits, he learned this from his father. Still, I really hoped, and I think we all did, that we were watching the actual outfall from some Hall Of Famer he encountered along the way.

So, in deference, Corey held the ball. The batter backed away from the plate and Cindy, hands on her hips, stood and stared. After all, Ed Zems had his own baseball card. This was a baseball game. And he was talking, we guessed, about baseball.

He turned to see Sam Alderdi stand and try to subtly wipe the tear from his 10-year-old tough-guy eyes. And then he twisted right back to Bobby.

"You know Linster," he shouted. "You know what the fucking score is now? It's 7-6 those bastards from Vermouth Concrete. It's the last fucking inning."

Under my breath, I whispered across the infield, "You idiot! Try harder!"

Bobby gave me his dumb smile, the one that says, "True, guilty, sorry." I'd seen it before. That's how you know a friend.

Zems glared at the other bench, then back at Bobby.

"You know Bobby, we've lost three games in a row because of you. Yeah, that's right, I'm pointing at you Bobby Linster. You are the worst player on this whole goddamn team, and you only play because these other idiots make me keep you on the team. And for what? So you can sell our ballfield?"

Zems turned away and then turned back to Bobby, "You should have talked to me."

Then Charlie turned to Bobby from first base and said, "He's right. You ruined everything."

The next batter hit the ball right at Charlie who performed a live replay of Bobby's error.

Gould yelled encouragement from third base, "That's all right!"

Then Zems and Bobby both shouted, "Shut up James!"

9

BALLOONS

Lisa threw a dart that wobbled mid-air and missed the navy blue balloon by an inch.

"I'm gonna try again," she said.

She pushed two more dollars to the short round bespectacled church lady. The lady wrinkled her face into a smile and handed back three more darts. Across the yard of St. Joseph's, I heard a local band called Firecracker announce they were about to play "American Woman."

"Good luck," said the fat woman again, just as she did the first time when Lisa had no luck. Again, all three darts wobbled and missed.

I laughed and kissed Lisa.

"At least our softballs don't wobble when you throw them," I said.

Firecracker was mangling the song. Then mid-song, it got louder. And the beat was off slightly so that I wanted to start singing in my head before the singer actually started singing. The noise gave me a headache. When the singer and my brain didn't coordinate on the song, it got worse. The pounding was ratcheted up by the lack of synchronicity. As we walked and the music overwhelmed my hurting synapses, seeming to grow even louder, I thought there should be some kind of law. If you are a band playing an overdone cover you should learn to play it right before going in public. Under penalty of torture, I thought. That's what this was, torture.

We pushed our way past a table of graying men in golf shirts eating hot dogs with their flabby-armed wives. Just as the song ended, we heard one of the men say, "I'm going to get a job at the baseball stadium. I bet it will be fun."

The woman across from him said, "Oh, Bill. They're gonna want young men."

He laughed. "Not on the team, Betty." All the men at the table laughed.

Mission as a concept had gained momentum. The churchyard was awash with orange and navy blue balloons. Vermouth as a prim ancient New England society, did its very best to jump through hoops. This church festival was held in honor of Peter Junkin and his plan to transform the town.

The *Messenger* did its part too, with banner headlines and continual joyful introductions. "Mission Will Be Vermouth's Shangri-La," said one of its over-the-top headlines. This is not surprising as the *Messenger* always runs on hyperbole. Once, the *Messenger* ran the banner, "Vermouth will not host the Olympics," as if there had been some realistic chance.

The next song started as a blast of electronics that turned into something that a gifted anthropologist might be able to listen to and say, "That's 'Born To Be Wild.'" I looked at Lisa and she looked back with the same eye-rolling expression. I nodded my head toward the property's edge, where a rope carrying navy blue and orange triangular

Brian Tarcy

flags and a sign saying, "Vermouth Welcomes Mission" hung over the driveway. We started walking but about 15 seconds into the song, as others seemed to stream in the same direction, the noise level dropped as if off a cliff. It fell all the way down to background noise.

"Well," I said to Lisa. The sound of the band disappeared completely.

"Well," she said, "let's stay for a while. I want to go on the Ferris Wheel."

But before we made it to the Ferris Wheel, Peter Junkin took to the stage with giant charts and graphs. And on a banner behind him was the new logo for Mission, a giant orange-and-blue M that seemed, maybe only to me, that the peaks of the "M" resembled devil's horns.

When he finished with the charts and graphs, Peter Junkin said, "That is just a small sample of what you and I can do together."

He had had a strong jaw and a bald crown surrounded by a ring of blond hair. He wore a shiny white shirt, rolled up at the sleeves.

"Look around everyone. Smile at your neighbor. Smile at this wonderful town you have built. Now, think to the future, a wonderful future with a new development that will put you on the map."

"Will there be jobs?" someone shouted. It sounded like an old man, maybe one of the graying golfers.

"I'm glad you asked that," said the man at the podium.

Folks have been talking about jobs forever in Vermouth, even longer than they've been talking about water. It is another one of those subjects that gets people like Selectman Cindy Morris and businessman Ed Zems all excited. There is a peculiar kind of power to the word "jobs." That's because no one around here—well except me, obviously—has a good one.

So, when Peter Junkin stood at the podium, his promises were inviting. He talked about the baseball stadium, the construction jobs (always a winner in Vermouth), and the possibility of luring high tech companies to operate in a corner of the property. Briefly, he mentioned the huge mall and the water park, but mostly he talked as though Bill Gates or someone like him was planning to move a thriving technology enterprise for the honor of locating in Mission.

"That would be great," said a kid holding a skateboard.

There must have been 500 people at the fair at any one time. While Junkin spoke, the Ferris Wheel stopped running, the music paused and even the food lines were closed. And the amplification kept getting louder until it almost matched that of Firecracker screeching, "Twist & Shout."

He babbled on about all the great things we could expect in our town. He hinted that celebrities "bigger than our own Ed Zems" would find our town soon enough. He hinted that we were all going to get rich. He explained the balloons by saying orange was his wife's favorite color and blue was his.

"This is going to be a family affair folks. You're all part of the family."

As we left, with Lisa clutching an orange balloon, I said that maybe this would give me a chance to be rich. Lisa shook her head and said, "I don't know."

We walked in the crowd for a bit and when we reached the front of the property, on the sidewalk, we saw three people carrying signs that said, in orange, "Mission Will Kill," and in blue, "An Endangered Species."

We slowed down.

One of the sign holders, a frumpy woman with oversized glasses said, "Do you know about the Red Cranial Woodpecker?"

We kept walking. She stood her ground, introduced herself as Victoria Manchester, and kept talking. It didn't matter who heard what portion of what sentence, this woman was insistent.

"The Woodpecker is endangered by this massive development. Please vote against Issue One in September. If this is allowed to go forward..."

Brian Tarcy

As we got out of hearing distance of the woman, Lisa let go of her orange balloon and it floated off towards the Ferris Wheel.

"Cletis," she said, "do you care about the Red Cranial Woodpecker?"

"Of course I care," I said. "I'm going to go home right now and make a sign. I bet that will help."

Lisa, missing what I thought was obvious sarcasm, said, "Well, I don't care at all."

"Okay, me either," I said.

10

THE MOON & STARS STRATEGY

We were in the Wild Bird after a game and I told Zerck that I'd run into Victoria Manchester, who, despite the size of Vermouth, I'd never actually seen before.

"I think we hang out at different places," I said.

"Victoria Manchester," said Zerck, "is the reason I have an unlisted phone number. She's been around forever."

I was thinking how I'd seen her name in the *Messenger* many times, but I never once actually read anything about her other than forgettable headlines until one week earlier. Despite my prodigious garbage reading, I have an aversion to local news because it all looks like gossip, and I was told as a small child that gossip is bad. Unlike everyone else in the world, I still believed it. The rub is that I have found it's hard work to be ignorant. But when I try, I am rather good at it.

"Back when I was a reporter" continued Zerck, "she used to call me at 8 in the morning on Saturdays to discuss my stories."

"I remember that," I said, remembering when he got his unlisted phone number.

I thought about this frumpy old woman calling Zerck at 8 on a Saturday morning. Now that was funny. It was about the worst strategy to approach him. If, by chance, he were able to stumble to the phone and mouth the word, "Hello," he would still only be able to say only one other sentence, "I'll call you later." Then, if she were lucky, he might remember to call later. Even if he did remembered, he still might not call.

Calling Zerck at 8 on Saturday morning. I think this alone made me like Victoria Manchester, who probably rang him at least once while he was still awake from the night before and thus, ramble-on-talkative and surely less than lucid. I bet you could sell the tapes, if they existed.

"She's single minded," he said. "I mean, she doesn't care about anything except what she cares about."

It was Wednesday night, August 1, and we were in the Bird after another loss. This time we lost 19-14, and at least we made a good comeback at the end. It had been a month since Bobby announced his good fortune to us, in that time his good fortune turned into our losing streak. We dropped to third place.

So, in between the beers and our bickering about baseball dropped the protestations of Victoria Manchester, who had become the talk of the town when she first appeared with her Red Cranial Woodpecker signs outside the grounds of St. Joseph's churchyard.

"Man, every town has a Victoria Manchester, a busybody who is also so moral that she is most always right," said Zerck. He was off on a rant against morality, one of his favorite subjects. He scratched his head. "She is right. But you know what?"

I waited for an answer. Zerck gulped his beer and rubbed his chin. He bit his lip, then drank more beer. He looked around the Bird. We were the only two there since Charlie and Alex abandoned us, and

Bobby, since it was a Wednesday, had to work that night.

"I don't care that she's right," Zerck finally said. "Busybody, I'm telling you. She's a damn busybody."

"What does Cindy think of her?" I asked.

"Well, Cindy needs her. That's her base. Victoria Manchester and her ilk."

"There are others like her?"

"Well, no. I mean, yes. I mean no one else is like Victoria. But, you know, the conservation types. Tree huggers and such. That's who votes for Cindy 'round here."

"Well there must be enough of them then," I said. "After all, Cindy's been elected twice."

"Four times actually."

"I don't pay attention," I said. "I mean, I sure try not to pay attention."

"You should."

"Yeah, you always say that. But you haven't given me a good reason yet."

Zerck grinned, "That's cause I don't have one. I just know you should."

"You just want me to buy your newspaper," I said.

"No more than you want me throw out my garbage," he said.

"Touché. Well then why?" I asked. "Why is it important for me to pay attention?"

That was when I finally won our ancient argument.

"I guess it's not," he said. "I guess it's not important at all."

"I knew it!" I said. "Ignorance *is* bliss."

But the victory felt sort of hollow because I actually knew, this time, he was right. I probably should pay attention. Then, Jane the bartender came over and we ordered another round and I forgot all about not paying attention.

Victoria Manchester, it turned out, was a former member of the planning board. She had served for 20 years before losing to a builder, a rival of Gould named Alan Patterson. If I ever read or remembered beyond headlines I would have known all of this. But I didn't know any of this until almost midnight when Zerck began giving me a civic education that I was too drunk to say I didn't want.

Zerck explained that she first surfaced as a loudmouth trying to change kindergarten curriculum.

"The earliest *Messenger* clips I found in the library described her as an activist for various causes," said Zerck, "and if you saw pictures of her from back then, even when she was a young woman she looked frumpy, just like now."

So Victoria Manchester, young and frumpy, formed or joined a handful of different organizations dedicated to this or that liberal cause until she finally found her calling, by mistake, in the cause of land use in Vermouth.

"She totally credits the bumper sticker, 'Think Globally, Act Locally' in her life-changing decision," said Zerck.

It was in an organization she founded—Land On Cape Cod or LOCC, that Victoria gave her a name and gained the platform with which to win a planning board seat. Then, once she was elected, she spent two decades badgering every developer, good and bad, into making changes to their plans. She tortured them using the machinations of zoning and planning. She was adept at also annoying her fellow board members whether they were decent like Ernie Johnson who was always known as Doctor Johnson, or wild-eyed pro-development types like Ed Zems who actually served one rambunctious term on the board and would have approved neon skyscrapers.

At first, her questions made great sense, said Zerck, but soon developers learned that no matter how good and responsible their plan was, Victoria Manchester would always demand more. So the standard strategy for all developers, became to ask for the moon and the stars and settle for most of the earth. Then, Zerck dropped a bit of great and even personal gossip. The moon-and-stars strategy to deal with Victoria Manchester was dreamt up by Joe Morris, Cindy's ex.

Last call came from Jane just as Zerck was telling me about what the paper's reporters had learned about the discovery of the Red Cranial Woodpecker near Mission Pond.

In 1934, Herman Gihrton, a birder from South Carolina was honeymooning in Vermouth. Herman Gihrton went inexplicably for a walk along Mission Pond when he saw the yellow flowers and didn't think a thing of it until he heard the familiar *tsssk tsssk tsssk* of the Red Cranial Woodpecker, a sound he grew up with in South Carolina. He knew immediately, of course.

We knew immediately to order one final round at last call.

And when the Mission project was announced, Victoria Manchester knew immediately that the Red Cranial Woodpecker was her biggest weapon—a symbolic type of cannon that seemed a fitting match to her ability to rankle.

"Yeah, the Red Cranial Woodpecker is big news to Victoria," said Zerck. "She'll use this. She'll be great. You saw. She's relentless, almost legendary. I'm telling you she will ride this bird until either she or it dies," he said. Then he added, "And she'll never die."

"Why is that?" I asked.

Zerck grinned maliciously.

"I believe she has no soul," he said.

"But neither do you," I countered.

"Never mind about that."

Brian Tarcy

11

RED CRANIAL WOODPECKER

Alex was fined $50 for living on the wrong side of the street on August 5th. It's logically true. When he turned the sprocket on his sprinkler that day, he was disobeying a town water ordinance that said folks on his side of the street could only water lawns on even-numbered days of the month. For that day, he was a water criminal.

The true water criminals, said Cindy, are the developers adding water consumption to the town while putting polluted water back into the ground. Zerck said the real criminals are joggers because they drink more water than everyone else does. Lisa sided with Cindy but was more specific. She said Peter Junkin was the problem, while I boldly proclaimed that the real culprit in all of our water woes was the Red Cranial Woodpecker. Bobby blamed God for not making it rain enough.

We were all at Alex's house when the police car stopped by. Alex was having a pre-game lunchtime barbecue. We were scheduled for a 3 o'clock game against Really Real Estate, and Alex had scored some illegal summertime venison from a poacher friend of his. We didn't ask questions, but I did wonder how he met this friend—at the poacher bar? Alex always had some strange alliances that kept him skirting the law in strange and vaguely moral ways. He didn't break laws that would have upset any of us. If there were a three-strikes rule, though, he would have been out—serving a life sentence as a career criminal. He cheated on his taxes, served and ate illegal venison and now, he had been caught watering his grass on August 5th.

The two young cops were polite and left quickly. As they drove away, Alex crumpled the ticket and tossed it into the fire.

"Rules!" he said to no one and to all of us. "You know! Who needs all this fucking bureaucracy?" He was looking right at Cindy. "I want it to be how it used to be. Can't even goddamn water my lawn. It's crazy. They fined me! Fifty bucks, can you believe it?"

We all knew they fined him of course. We witnessed it, and yet. I at least understood this frustration with rules. When a small town with no real rules to speak of suddenly becomes a big town with the kind of rules needed to control a large group of people, the old ways go out the window. The old Vermouth was gone. Disappeared when we weren't even looking and then we looked and it was gone. All gone or going; disappearing even right here in Alex's house.

Living within the rules has never been a strong point of any of our gang, not even Cindy when I think about it. By the mere act of playing on the Townies team, Cindy is flouting a whole bunch of conventions, a politician hanging out with the likes of us being the most obvious.

In my overwrought yet simplistic analysis of why none of us had a ton of respect for authority, the best explanation I could come up with is that, as young children, we witnessed our older siblings sing protest songs and march against those they called corrupt and powerful. We absorbed everything. I used to be jealous of the generation in front of me but now they're old and we're not quite, so at least that's something.

That's what I was thinking when Cindy jumped up. She knew Alex was talking about her when he ranted against rules. Cindy was funny that way. She took her job, her *politics* serious.

"You know, Alex," she said.

"Yes, I know," he said. "I'm not stupid. But c'mon, what I did does not warrant a fifty dollar fine."

I had to agree. So did Bobby and Zerck.

Poor Cindy. She placed herself in the position of defending this fine when she jumped up. As a town father she was formally, though disconnectedly, connected to the fine.

She said, "You're right, but you're wrong." And then she went into a long dissertation on a subject that we all knew about and had heard before—how everything in nature is connected.

Even though we had all heard it before, Cindy had a funny forceful Zen way of testifying. If you believed what she had to say, her roller coaster delivery was nearly spellbinding, and if you didn't, at least the grating parts were passionate. As a politician, she had flashes of the gift. So when the water on Alex's lawn became connected to the polluted water in South Vermouth and to the splash-filled waters of Mission Pond, Cindy's voice became louder, and sometimes poetic.

The subject of the $50 fine had long since disappeared into the ether. Zerck was beaming.

I decided the night before. Well, Lisa and I decided. Well, Lisa decided and I decided to agree with her. Anyway, the decision was this: I was going to quit the garbage route when I could. I was going to try to get a job at the new minor league baseball stadium.

Lisa and I decided during pillow talk.

"It's all changing, Cletis," she said.

It was all we ever talked about lately. Change, this Mission thing, it had taken over as a *topic*. I listened. She talked about the future of the town, and she was naked. Plus she was beautiful when she said the development gave her job security since more people would be moving here, producing more kindergarten kids. I said it would give me job security too.

She laughed, looking really pretty.

"You're not going to be a garbage man forever, are you?"

I'd known her since I was eight. She was my friend. I thought that no one is any different. Money and prestige—I have none and Lisa, like everybody, wants some. Yet I underestimated her. Again. I looked and remembered. She just did *that* with me. Plus, get this—she insisted that *she liked it*. Although I was 40 and had done it more than once in my time, I was still amazed by all the circumstances and texture-like feelings associated with sex. Nothing was more real, or surreal. And Lisa, gosh. I definitely liked her. It wasn't just her insane panther-like approach to sex. I liked her. I loved her eyes when she looked at me like that. It felt so good as to almost be impossible. So I surprised myself. I brought up those old guys at the Mission Fair at St. Joseph's and how I figured I could out hustle them.

She told me I was so smart.

For two weeks, Victoria Manchester put it everywhere around the town. In the *Messenger*, I saw pictures and stories and even published scientific studies. On the street by the newly opened office of Junkin Associates, there were protesters with signs and protesters across from the protesters, protesting against the protesters. It slowed the already-slow tourist traffic. Then, Victoria Manchester announced she was writing a book about the bird.

Brian Tarcy

The Red Cranial Woodpecker became Vermouth's very own catchy ditty that you couldn't get out of your head. On public access television, a half-hour special aired, starting with the story of Herman Gihrton's honeymoon and finishing with a detailed analysis of the Hellfire Hawkweed growing around Mission Pond. At the Wild Bird the night before, Jane brought over our beer along with a brochure from the National Audubon Society.

"Don't tell Corey I gave this to you," she said. "But it's important."

That's why I took to blaming the Red Cranial Woodpecker for everything. On Monday, I was missing a sock and it was the fault of the Red Cranial Woodpecker. On Tuesday, there was a plane crash in Argentina and the Red Cranial Woodpecker was the obvious cause. On Wednesday the bird wreaked havoc on the stock market, and on Thursday—and seemingly everyday—the Red Cranial Woodpecker caused old-age problems for my old blue Chevy.

12

DREAMER'S ROW

Pop fly to me. Great way to end this slaughter so I hot-dogged it and flipped my glove through the ball to pull it in, as a shortstop showoff move. This was fun, athletic outdoor kind of fun, the kind that I kept reminding myself that I always had at the same place where I had always had it. It was not yet the backdrop to a mall and I tried to think that I didn't care because I was winning again and that was a lot more important than I jokingly pretended it was. Yeah, pop fly to me. How important was winning?

Yes. Well, yes. A two-game winning streak was a breakthrough for the Townies and I was proud of us for pulling though. We let our athletic ability come to the front and despite what Zems said—it was funny about Zems and his pro baseball ability to motivate—we were coming together as a team.

He didn't want it. Hell, as we splintered who did? But it didn't matter what any of us wanted because, despite our intentions, we played well, really well, for one inning, then another, then for two straight games. In the first eight innings of the game while we were figuring it out, we were losing 19-0. Then, remarkably, we brought it to 19-14 in the last inning. And since then we had been on a two-game tear. Normally a two-game streak would not be considered a tear, but this was really a roll that felt oddly unstoppable, mostly because the other roll was so bad. Funny, how it goes. It started innocently enough.

It was 19-0. It was the ninth inning. Zems walked past us bragging that he hated the entire team, the entire world, and all living creatures in the universe.

"I hate you guys," he said. "This is horrible. I hate everyone, everything. You know what I hate?" There were two outs and no one was on base. Bobby was at bat. "You guys make me hate puppies. You suck!" yelled Zems at Bobby. "You all suck!" yelled Zems at the bench. "We suck!" he shouted at the sky. "I suck!" he emphasized. "This is the worst team in the history of..." Then he just stopped, as if he couldn't think of a history large enough.

Bobby smacked the ball over the shortstop for a double in the gap. It was insane, of course, to think it but I thought it I swear. Later no one believed me, not even me really. But it's true. When Bobby hit the ball I believed we were going to win.

We had two outs, only down by 19.

We scored 13 straight runs, slapping the ball and running past tags like a bad cliché, like a rock and roll movie, like a cartoon. One hit after another until we were jumping on each other and Zems was the biggest of all the cheerleaders. Thirteen runs without an out! Then Zerck hit the longest possible line drive you can hit without it disappearing into the marsh. It went to deep left center field. And when the center fielder tracked it down, Alex had run from second all the way to home. Zerck rounded second. The outfielder threw it to the shortstop. Zerck dug for third. The throw was lightening quick. Zerck slid. And Zerck was out.

But it was the beginning of a two-game roll that felt as powerful as any experience in all of my years in team sports. I wanted to believe this. So after I hauled in the pop fly, and we won 27-2 over Really Real Estate that Saturday afternoon, I thought that maybe this moment was the athletic peak of my life. I needed to savor it.

I've always worried about missing my athletic peak and I didn't think I ever really had one before even though I have always been pretty good. But, a peak means a lot of things, including that it's all downhill from there. Still, a peak also implies the height of greatness and well, we won 27-2. I didn't know. I went through all the post-game motions and pondered all of this.

Someone said, "Here Cletis."

"It's happening," said Gould. "It's happening again. Today was great, huh?"

We were in his poolroom. Zerck was there with Cindy, I was with Lisa, and Gould was with his rarely seen, beautiful wife, Leslie. Gould lined a straight-on shot at the 14-ball into the far corner. Led Zeppelin's "Whole Lotta Love" played in the background and in the opening riffs I found my body twinge with thoughts of air guitar. I stifled the thought inside my middle-aged brain, instead agreeing with Gould that things seemed to be coming together for the Townies.

The stupid losing streak and the accompanying bitching had begun to make the whole idea of this team seem more of a nuisance than a hobby. But after we had scored 14 runs in one inning, then two days later demolished Lazy Lobster Restaurant, and this afternoon destroyed Really Real Estate I started to find it fun again. Hitting, running, scoring, cheering—that was fun.

Brian Tarcy

"Yeah, it's fun again," I said.

Gould took his shot and missed, kissing the ball just slightly off center so that it bounced back to almost where it was before.

"Shit!" said Gould to the table. Then, to me, "It *is* fun again. Baseball. You know. Despite it all, it's still baseball."

"Yeah, when it is just baseball," said Cindy. She was right, of course. Recently, it seemed our gatherings were not primarily to play a game but instead to theatrically argue. And some were better at arguing than others, just as some were better at baseball.

"Look Cindy," said Gould, "I'm just trying to keep the team together."

"Hell of a way," she said, "getting involved with those people."

"Who?"

"You know damn well who!"

"Peter and Melissa?"

"Yes. The Junkins," she said as if she took special joy in the "junk" part of their last name.

"Yes, Peter and Melissa Junkin. They're good people who want to change this town for the better."

"Better? You wouldn't know better if it bit you on the leg," said Cindy, trying on some anger.

"Oh no?" said Gould. His face, his eyes, had a slight grin. "You know Cindy. Selectman Cindy," he said for effect, "I know better. You want to know how I know better? I know a lot of things and I know that Mission is the best thing that will happen to this town in our lifetimes. The absolute best."

I didn't have time to stop myself from blurting out what I was thinking. "What about our baseball team? Isn't that the best?"

Lisa lined up the 4-ball into the side pocket.

"You know what's feels perfect to me?" she asked. "Our baseball field. At least that's staying."

She smiled right at me. I watched the smile and knew it was

directed at me. That is the best feeling in the world, I thought. That's what feels perfect.

"We've been going there forever," she said.

"Perfect?" laughed Gould. "You know, there are very few places on Earth that are actually like that," said Gould, "but my house, man, this place really is perfect. I'm telling you guys. I got the dream."

We were in his dream house, a modern mansion with too many angles, stairs and mirrors.

"The place makes me seasick," was Alex's comment to me last year when he first saw the dream house that Gould built in East Vermouth. But Gould was proud and I could see that he was. Lisa thought that the only thing he loved more than his house was himself. I thought that was fair—both of Lisa and of Gould.

It was a tremendous house. Exhaustedly and through three previous houses, Gould had studied real estate in town and when this lot became available in East Vermouth, he'd pounced on it.

Through my garbage travels, I had noticed that there is something about Palmer Hills especially that compelled landowners to build one-upmanship houses. It went beyond the standard bragging with lumber that had become common all over the Cape. This was bragging with aggressively excessive architecture.

In Palmer Hills, there existed a row of six harebrained attempts at magnificence of ideas. Zems had his absurdly designed house, of course, and Gould had this modern monstrosity. In between was a house built half underground that connected perfectly into a tree-house living room with an ocean view. I loved visiting Palmer Hills. I hated doing the garbage there because it took so much getting in and out of the truck. The houses are so far apart that you couldn't walk but you didn't ride long enough to get comfortable. For a little stretch though, I got to visit what the *Messenger* called Dreamers' Row. Although Zems and Gould were friends of mine, and I knew one of the other owners too, I still thought the houses look like the houses of eccentric circus clowns.

One was simply built to look like an 1800s mansion, except that it was painted all the colors in the world. The craftsmanship on all of the shaped wood was top rate, and the painting was professional. Every color that has ever been invented was on the house somewhere, as if Jerry Garcia himself was there, selling LSD with a bullhorn. Now, the former owner of an Internet company owns it. This guy sold all his stock in some dotcom just before the company's stock dove. I met him once. His name is Charles Brewer. He asked me to not throw the garbage cans on his lawn. Gould told me that Brewer is hardly ever home and spends most of his time in the Caribbean, yet each week the psychedelic house produced an awful lot of stomach-turning garbage.

It had been a long day but we had decided the night before to stick around as the last guests to talk to Gould about the possibility of my getting a job at the baseball stadium. He said he had connections, maybe, the right ones to get me in the stadium. It had become an inside joke between Lisa and I already.

I looked at Lisa off to the side in the party and I said, "Hot dogs. Get your hot dogs here."

So when Zerck and Cindy left, Leslie said she was going to bed. Gould had tied one on pretty good but he was functional enough, I figured, to remember in the morning what we were about to talk about.

So, as Zerck and Cindy headed up his driveway to Cindy's massive dark blue Chevy Suburban, I said, "Before we leave, I've got a question for you, James."

"You don't have to leave. Come on back in. I'll grab you a beer. Put the game on."

"What game?" asked Lisa.

"I don't know. There's got to be a game on."

You Can't Sell Right Field   73

So Lisa and I each grabbed a side of the love seat and I found the remote control and clicked until I found an Atlanta Braves game. They were losing 4-3 to the Dodgers in the eighth inning.

Gould brought back beers for each of us. He sat in the chair across from us. I took a sip and put mine down.

"What's up Cletis?" he asked.

Lisa squeezed my knee.

"Well, I think I want a job at the new baseball stadium."

He looked at me, smiled and shook his head. He stood, touched his nose. He looked again. He sat back down.

Then he stood again and said, "Cletis." He chortled slightly and shook his head once more.

By now, Lisa was elbowing me. She gave me the "What-the?" look.

Gould sat back down. "You know, Cletis, it's funny about that. See, the thing is—well, I've got something like bad news. It's not supposed to be known until tomorrow, but Peter Junkin is scrapping the baseball stadium part of Mission because of the Red Cranial Woodpecker. You know, the habitat."

"Can they just scrap the whole project?" asked Lisa, leaning forward.

Gould laughed, "No. That's not going to happen," He turned and looked at me, "but look, if you want to be a garbage man at the mall, my offer still stands."

It was funny about Gould. He had always been like this, like some sort of silver-spooned monolith, a little different than those of us who grew up in Sandy Hills. But he had good enough qualities as to always be included and one of his good enough qualities was his insistence on being included. He, like Zems, was able to parlay the chips of nice houses and great parties into meaningful friendships. Time and shared experience created our friendships with him, even though he could sometimes say astonishing things like, *My offer still stands.*

"No thanks," I said. "I was really interested in the baseball stadium."

"Well, you never know," he said. "Things might change again. I'll keep you in mind, that's for sure."

We said our pleasant-enough good-byes and then Lisa and I walked to my car. It had started raining and that made me laugh. But three minutes later we were back at Gould's front door.

"Can I get a jump?" I asked. "My car won't start."

13

FREE TICKETS TO A TRAIN WRECK

I knew the effort required for remembering, and that, I guess, constitutes memory itself, therefore, maybe my ignorance was less than honest, but I swear I didn't really know that Victoria Manchester had challenged Peter Junkin to a debate about Issue One in the Sandy Hills Elementary School for that night. With more than a few million dollars at stake, depending on how the *Messenger* covered the event, Junkin accepted.

I found out when Bobby called me after work to ask if I wanted to get stoned and go watch it in person. Talk about an offer. This would indeed be high entertainment, so high that Bobby took the night off of work at the Ocean Market.

And that is why Bobby is my best friend. More than anyone else I know, he gets it. As dense and small-town-trailer-trash as he is—so says the garbage man—Bobby could be smarter than Aristotle sometimes.

It could be argued that the greater good is not served by indulging in intoxicating substances and laughing at the absurdity of important subjects, but Bobby would brilliantly counter-argue that the greater good is never served so he would like someone instead to simply serve him a beer.

And that is how we ended up going to the debate.

"I think it's going to be funny," said Bobby.

"No, they're going to pontificate on end," I said. "It could really be horrible, like history class in 10th grade."

"You don't know people, dude. You're a fucking garbage man," he said. "Here Cletis," he exhaled, "I deal with people all day long. I'm telling you, this is like getting free tickets to a train wreck."

You don't know arrogance unless you've seen arrogance. But there is something even more revealing—seeing arrogance battle against sanctity. Peter Junkin and Victoria Manchester were that. Wow, I had no idea.

And I thought that it was too bad that Zerck wasn't with us because he was the very best at ripping sanctity apart but he said he had something else to do that night. But Bobby was there and that was good enough for me because he thought arrogance was even funnier than sanctity. And in Bobby's context, Peter Junkin fit the bill of arrogant to a tee.

But he was much more than merely arrogant. He was a magician. It is possible, I learned from Junkin, to say the words "327 acres" with religious fervor. It is an incredible feat, one that definitely deserves the accompanying *hallelujah* that Bobby swore you could hear piped in from the heavens as Peter Junkin spoke. I agreed, and more. I'm not saying I thought the man had charisma. I am testifying.

We were sitting in the same cafeteria—the auditorium was closed for construction—where we used to eat lunch when we were in grade school. It made me feel incredibly old but oddly young again. There we were, neither young nor old, right in the middle of life. Sitting in the middle of that room, there was something bothering me, something about the pasty brick of the place that seemed to creep at me. The dramatic pitch of the debate increased with each exchange, but my mind was climbing inside the layers of paint on the walls—looking for the stories they could tell.

Mine were buried here—somewhere. Birds and baseball stadiums bounced around my ears for a bit, then I remembered the oddest thing. There was a girl in school that nobody liked. Her name was Gwen Pine. I don't know why I remembered her or how I even remembered her name, but I remembered how all the kids in school, including me, teased her and called her ugly. Until one year, I just decided it wasn't right and I started to be nice to her. I don't even know how or why I decided. It made sense back then to my child's brain, somehow.

The thing is, in retrospect, I was nominally nice at best. I'd say "hi" to her. I didn't call her ugly. I think that's it.

And I was so proud.

I flashed from that back to the debate.

Without thinking, I said, "The problem with Victoria Manchester is that she is right, horribly right, morally on some really solid ground," I said.

"Yeah, that bothers me too," said Bobby.

I scratched my head, thought a bit, then I decided to add, "The problem with Peter Junkin is that he has a lot of money."

"I don't see that as a problem," said Bobby. "I like money."

The problem with problems is that everyone talks about them. Why things can't just stay the same I'll never understand. Change seems to be the order of every day except those days when I am looking for change, and I literally mean change as in coins. But that's another story, this lack of money is a way of life.

Peter Junkin told a story. He told of a time a few weeks back when his wife went to Mission Pond, and she was greeted by the warmest Vermouth welcome she had ever seen, and she returned the welcome as best she could.

Bobby turned to me. "Didn't you tell me you guys saw her on Mission Pond?" he asked.

"She either got a warm greeting from someone else, some other time," I said, "or this guy is the most creative liar in North America."

"Do they have that award?"

Victoria Manchester then repeatedly used the word "historic" to make some point about conservation, before launching into another pompous monologue about the dwindling water supply and the endangered Red Cranial Woodpecker.

"There are other species that we don't even know about yet," she said. "When we find them, they could be endangered."

"If you don't know about them, how could they be endangered?" asked Junkin.

She smiled smugly.

"You know, I bet those species are hoping you don't find them and make them endangered," Junkin said.

"It's not about the birds," whispered Bobby to me. "It's about the humans. It's always about the humans."

"What are you talking about?" I whispered back.

"You think it's about the animals?"

I nodded.

"No. It's about the people who love the animals. To them, this is their money. This is like money is to Peter Junkin. That bird is currency, sort of."

"But how?"

"You don't get it, do you?"

"No, I mean, money is money, and a bird is a bird."

"As amazing as it sounds, money isn't the most important thing to some people."

"I don't believe you," I said.

"Frankly, I'm also shocked. But it's true. There are people who take more joy out of being in nature, even just knowing that nature exists than they could ever get from money."

"So saving the bird to these people is like winning the lottery would be to you or me?" I asked.

"Well, yeah, but no. It's deeper than that somehow," said Bobby. "I can't explain it, but I bet it's like church or something."

"Church?" I said. "That's funny."

But then I thought of my raft on Mission Pond. Church? Yeah, maybe a bird can do that for some people.

On stage, Victoria Manchester was speculating.

"As development continues to affect the entire town of Vermouth, the entire East Coast and in fact the entire world, who is to say this habitat might not be a refuge for any number of species? Maybe the geese that are there now will become endangered, or more likely, the Golden Throated Bullfrogs, which I've been told, are close to falling onto the endangered species list."

"The bird is like," said Bobby, "I don't know, kind of like kids or the ocean or God—a bigger concept to them."

"But it's not like the birds are going to die," I said. "It's just a lost tribe."

"Yeah, but if we kick them out, they become like bird refugees, and who needs to see more footage on the news of refugees huddled in some fenced in refugee camp."

"At least it wouldn't take much to feed them," I countered. "They eat like birds."

Victoria Manchester finished with a heartfelt plea. "I am begging all of you. Those of you who have lived here a long time and those of you who are new here. I'm begging you to recognize what you have."

She paused.

"I am begging you to vote against this zoning change on September 5," she said to a mixed reaction of clapping, cheers, hoots and boos. "This development has no place in this town. That land should never be developed. I'd even go a step further. I'd like to see that hideous ballpark at the front of the property get to grow over. That could be glorious habitat."

Peter Junkin slapped his hand lightly but noticeably on his podium and said, "Well, I'll be."

"You don't like baseball?" he asked.

"Not particularly."

"Well, you just made up my mind for me. As you know, I have been forced to redesign the project because of the Red Cranium Woodpecker. And I have been looking at two different options. One, as you may have heard, was to downsize and get rid of the plan for the baseball stadium. Well, that was the way I was leaning until tonight. I think a person such as you, Ms. Manchester, does more damage than good to her own cause. You see, you made me realize just how important baseball is to this project and to this town. So rather than downsize, I am going to move the entire project 400 feet. I am not going to sue. I am moving everything."

There was cheering. I cheered. Bobby watched.

"This will be the best baseball stadium of its size in the entire nation," said Junkin, "and the Red Cranium Woodpecker will live."

More cheering.

"The Red Cranial Woodpecker needs all the land that is there now," said Victoria Manchester, but she was already drowned out by the cheers.

"So please pass Issue One," continued Junkin, "and now I'd like to invite a comment from your esteemed selectman, Cindy Morris." I spun my head. So did Victoria Manchester.

"I would like to say that a new baseball stadium brings significant revenues to this town, and the infrastructure of the town will be strengthened by the required improvements and the voluntary ones Mr. Junkin has offered," said Cindy.

I saw Junkin smile at her.

"And by graciously agreeing to move the stadium without a battle for the sake of an endangered species, Mr. Junkin has shown that his plan is adaptable to local concerns," said Cindy. "Clearly, this project, with some slight revisions, is good for the town of Vermouth," said Cindy.

"I'd like to add something," came another familiar voice. Zerck! "Peter Junkin is the most professional and organized man I have ever met. He will do great things for this town," he said. "You've all seen the ads in the *Messenger*, I'm sure."

Then Cindy said, "The one concession the town is making is that we are eliminating that ball field to make room for the mall. Think of it as a tradeoff, a neighborhood ball field for a minor league stadium."

And there it was. The train wreck. Just as Bobby had foretold.

14

MARKET REVOLUTION

Alex said, "Maybe someday the sun won't rise in the east but as long as it does, I intend to run to first base on Mission Field."

"First base is going to be the underwear section at some fancy store," said Lisa.

"Shouldn't that be second base?" I asked.

"Or third?" said Charlie with a smile.

"No," said Alex. "First base is going to be a base."

When Alex suggested we bring the idea to Bobby at the Ocean Market, I tipped Jane three bucks, encouraged Charlie to do the same, and held Lisa's hand. Let the record show that we left the Wild Bird at 1 a.m. on August 19 as a group of old friends. An hour later, joining with Bobby, we had become a political movement.

In the large scheme, I guess it's only a baseball field. But my life had never changed before. Well, I mean besides graduation, marriage, divorce, and my garbage job. But somehow, much to my dismay, I found that I was part of the cosmos—connected and feeling a bit scared. It certainly wasn't fair.

Bobby was making subs at a frantic pace for all the after-hour drunks. We got in line. "Hey," he yelled. "What are you guys doing here?"

"Shut up and keep making sandwiches," said Charlie.

"Okay sir, and how much arsenic would you like on yours?"

This got a good laugh from all the after-hour drunks who turned and looked at us and tried to figure out what four middle-aged people were doing out at the spawning hour.

Charlie entertained them with off-color banter about the lollipops on the counter and this took some heat off of Bobby, who was slapping meat and mustard around with NASCAR-like speed.

When the other drunks left the building, Alex told Bobby to skip our sandwiches, take a break and join us outside for a cigarette. Bobby didn't smoke. None of us did. But at the Ocean Market, Bobby was allowed to take a "cigarette break" whenever the store was empty and he needed a smoke.

So, rules being rules, Bobby grabbed his pack of cigarettes and took a break. He always kept a pack at the store, in case Joe Bursetti, his boss, showed up and asked what he was doing outside.

At this point, he was leaning against the dirty white wood of the old building, drinking a lemon-lime Gatorade. But there was no boss showing up. It was 2 a.m. Instead, we were there and Alex began.

"We've been talking, Bobby," he said, "and, well, we've been talking about, you know, the situation with the land out there by Mission Pond."

"Look!" Bobby suddenly snorted. He bounced up. "Can you guys just leave me the fuck alone already? It's done! There's nothing I can do anymore. Fuck!"

"Bobby," said Lisa.

"No really, just go away. Okay. I don't need your drunken shit."

"But Bobby," I said.

"Go!" said Bobby.

"We're gonna try and win the election," said Charlie with great glee at finally being able to get to the point.

"What?"

"Do you remember Issue One?" I asked.

"That's what we've been trying to tell you," said Alex. "We've been talking and we finally decided to quit blaming you."

"Thank you."

"But what we decided is to join up and participate in the democracy."

"You can't do that," said Bobby.

"Why not?" I asked.

"Look at you. Look at all of us."

"So?" said Alex as only he could—expressing astonishment that anyone would think anything of him other than admiration.

"What can we do?" asked Bobby, echoing what we all said to Alex earlier in the evening.

Alex said the same thing to Bobby that he said to us.

"Well, we can do nothing and see if that works."

When you live in the same town all your life, every place brings you back in time and yet none of them do anymore because they are all so familiar. Schools especially take you back, because you don't go in them again unless your kids do. But other places do too, like the ball field, Mission Pond, and Market Beach, which are always capable of giving me a ticket on the time train. Still, the place that somehow does it for me every time is the Ocean Market. Especially on the rare occasions recently when I come in late at night and see Bobby working.

When we were 16, we took jobs at the old market. Charlie had already been working there for two years when Bobby, Zerck, Alex and I started working for Mike Campbell, the owner, three owners ago. If I was to do some sort analysis of the summers of my life up to my 40th I would have to say that the 16th may have been the best ever. It was amazing that we all didn't get fired, and, in retrospect, sort of funny— the things that made me happy. It was youth, I guess. I glowed inside, and it hurt good, like a first hangover— also part of that summer.

"Doing something," Bobby argued bravely for the concept of cowardice, "requires putting yourself into the world. Do you really want to do that?"

"People judge you all the time anyway," said Alex, who seemed to have prepared more mentally for this late night argument with Bobby than he ever did as a lawyer for a client.

"Yeah, but they judge me as a store clerk. No one much cares about my opinions. But putting myself—ourselves—out into the world? Are you crazy? People like us don't have a right in something this big." Bobby reached in his pocket and pulled out a cigarette. "I gave away that right when I sold that land. Okay. I said it."

"People like us?" I asked, incredulous. I'd never thought of it before, but he was right. Still, I couldn't stop despite myself. "Who are people like us? What the hell are you talking about?"

"You know, people..." he sighed, trying to think but ultimately only coming up with, "like us. Look around, man. We're everywhere. Dumb working stiffs. We have no power." It was true, of course. "You guys are just pissed because I sold the land. I don't blame you." He pointed his cigarette at me.

Alex grabbed the cigarette from Bobby's hand and threw it on the ground. "We've moved on, Bobby. You don't understand."

"I think you'll be surprised," I said. "We're really going to try to stop this thing."

Bobby slid his hands into his pockets.

"You see, Bobby," said Lisa, "there are less than three weeks left until the town votes on that zoning change."

"Issue One," I said.

"Yeah, but first of all no one cares and if they do care they're in favor of this thing," said Bobby.

"We're not," said Alex.

"What about Zerck and Cindy?"

"What about them?" I asked.

"If they're in favor of this development, then almost everybody is because those two are never in favor of any development," said Bobby.

"They must be on the take," Lisa said.

"It's the baseball stadium," I speculated. I don't know why I suddenly thought I'd figured it all out. But I was sure, as I could physically feel the anger grind inside of me, that Zerck and Cindy had fingerprints all over the sudden change in plans. I tried to sort through my anger—it was mostly toward them, at what seemed a faded or fading friendship, than it was at the loss of the field. That anger, I knew, would keep building. But this group tonight—these were friends. My stomach muscles cringed. "Something's up Bobby," I said.

"The problem is Peter Junkin is offering to the town something really incredible when you think about it," said Bobby.

"I've thought about it," said Alex, turning to me, "and you know what he's offering? He's offering to take my town away from me and to build a new one for himself. He's taking Vermouth away."

"I think it's the Red Cranial Woodpecker's fault," I said.

My first job during my 16th summer was hauling cardboard boxes around the Ocean Market to repeatedly stock the shelves with cans upon cans of alleged food products. Charlie trained us and berated us and even got on our case about how often we were using the restroom. He made it painfully clear that he took great joy being in charge of four knuckleheads from his neighborhood. He studied our time cards each week, and stood guard by the time clock each morning as we arrived. One week into the job, we realized that Charlie was a way more obnoxious boss than he was a teammate and neighbor. By that time we had been caught sneaking the Finn twins into the milk cooler for a game of find the stick of butter, and he astonishingly let it slide. So we accepted his advice and cooled it. When Charlie was promoted from chief clerk and stock boy to assistant manager in the middle of that summer, we had freer reign in Mike Campbell's store.

Charlie has always been the most obnoxious of all my friends. He also has the biggest heart, willing to sacrifice anything for anyone who is close to him. That summer, for instance, he sacrificed his job for Alex. Alex got caught stealing beer from the store and Charlie, for some reason, told Mike Campbell that he had given Alex permission to take the beer. Charlie was immediately fired.

That was the only bad thing that happened that summer, and it didn't happen until the very end.

When Charlie was fired the first week in September, we at first were all relieved to be rid of him. But then the oddest thing happened—it may have had to do with the fact that it was September and we were no longer summer employees or that it was no longer summer or that we now had school responsibilities—it felt different. We weren't having fun any more, and I always thought that it might have been because Charlie wasn't around to make sure we could.

We talked for two hours. Three groups of customers pulled in during that time and each time we paused our town-saving seminar so Bobby could play a super hero of a different kind—Subman sometimes, Nicotineman others.

The first group that pulled in was composed of two lithe young women in a white VW Jetta with a front bumper that looked like it was falling off. They wore tight clothes that matched with their gum-chewing giggly demeanors. Bobby went in the store first, followed by the girls and then Charlie.

"Hey Mr. Alderdi," said the shorter of the two. "Funny to see you out this late at night."

Charlie stumbled with his intentions and came around to, "Oh, hey. Yeah, well." They walked in the door and he walked back out.

"One way or another," he laughed, "my kids keep me in line."

"Friends of Mary's?" asked Lisa.

"I guess so."

Inside, Bobby made two Italian subs, one without hot peppers. Out by the front of the building, Alex asked us how he thought we were doing.

"We've been talking for 20 minutes and we haven't even convinced, Bobby," I offered. "How do we expect to convince anybody in town?"

"We don't have to convince people in town to work against this. We're going to do all the work," said Alex.

"I don't get it," said Charlie. "How exactly are we going to work?"

"It's politics, Charlie. It's a whole new game for us," said Alex. "We're making things up as we go."

"But we're going to make it happen," I said stubbornly.

The girls came out with their subs and said their good-byes to Charlie. They climbed in their car and drove away as the fan belt squealed.

Bobby came out again and said, "Okay, I'm in. So, how are we going to save our baseball field? What's our plan?"

Bobby said he came around to our idea in the middle of the pro-volone on the second sub. "This will be like old times," he said.

"Not exactly," said Lisa. "This will actually be serious."

The second car to pull into the lot was a blue Cadillac, much like Zems' car. Again, in went Bobby, but this time only the passenger got out of the car and it was a wrinkled man in a golf shirt. His wife, stayed in the car, which was running and, the man made sure— looking at us—locked.

The old man returned with a roll of toilet paper, which prompted Charlie to do a too-long monologue about what these two had been doing just before they drove to the Ocean Market at 2 a.m. to buy one roll of toilet paper.

"They must have been wiped out," he said, as we knew he would.

After the old toilet paper couple left and the monologue had its badda-bing moment, Charlie fell silent. Bobby was back, having heard the end of Charlie's toilet paper riff. Now, all we could hear was the ocean. We could see the empty beach parking lot from the Ocean Market. The beach seemed empty of people. We just heard soft waves churning, over and over. Then Charlie stood up.

"So, you guys have thrown around a lot of ideas, but we in the electronics business like to put things in writing so we know exactly what we've bought or sold," he said.

"What are you talking about Charlie?" asked Alex.

I had to admit I was perplexed too.

"The way you draw up a plan is to actually draw up a plan," said Charlie.

Wait a minute! This was actually right and it was Charlie suggesting the most obvious of things to us, who could not see the obvious.

"Charlie's right," said Bobby. "If we're going to try to win an election, and there are only us, then we are going to need to figure out a way and then trust each other to do our duties."

"There's more than just us," said Charlie, again stating the obvious. "Lots of people don't want this, you know. There's the whole baseball league, for one." He paused.

"And Victoria Manchester and the bird people too," I said. "We have to work together."

"Like a baseball team," said Lisa.

"Like a winning baseball team," I countered.

We talked a little of softball, of our team, our youth and what exactly we were trying to save.

"I still remember where the best hiding place is for hide-and-seek," I said.

"Where?" asked Charlie.

"I'm not telling you. What if we play again?"

"I know where it is," said Alex. "It's by the big boulder off to the left on the path to the pond."

"That's a good guess, but you don't know where by the big boulder."

"I'm sure I'd find you," said Alex.

"Me too," said Charlie. "I know where you mean."

But we weren't there, talking to Bobby, for nostalgia's sake. We were seeking revolution.

So we did the most corporate thing we could think of. We agreed during our meeting to have another meeting. First, we agreed that we were committed to stopping Mission, then we scheduled a meeting for the following evening after the game to discuss it further. We agreed, friends forever, above all else. We were fully behind this cause. We could actually change the mind of an entire town about something worth millions of dollars. Our on the spot slogan, dreamt up by Charlie, was *Question 1 Ruins The Fun.*

"I think we can win this," said Bobby. "I actually do."

"Me too," said Alex.

The third car that pulled in was silver Nissan Sentra. Driving it was a young man in back-and-white waiter garb complete with a bow tie.

"Hey," he said to Bobby, who entered the store first.

Though he didn't look the part, for that night this young waiter was the Marlboro man. He came out the door and immediately lit one.

He started walking to his car when Alex said, "Hey, got a minute?"

"The sun's going to be coming up sooner than I want, man. What do you want?"

"You a resident of the town?"

"Yeah, born and raised."

"Cool. Us too. Listen, do you know anything about that Mission project?"

"Oh yeah, I heard about it. I heard it's going to be awesome."

Alex stood slack jawed.

"So," said the waiter after a moment, "is that it?"

"Well, it's not gonna be awesome," said Alex. "It's gonna ruin everything."

"That so?"

"Yeah."

"How do you know? I mean, aren't they saving that bird? That's what my Dad says. He says they're saving the bird because they have to and the rest doesn't matter."

"But..." Alex started.

The young man interrupted him. "Look man. I just want a better job. If this brings me a better job, I want it."

15

MEETING ON THE PITCHER'S MOUND

Gorman's Landscaping was in first place before the 3 p.m. game on the afternoon of Sunday, August 20. We had clawed our way back into second, one game back, with one week left in the season. From there, we would head to the playoffs.

So, with one week to go and our chance at a first round playoff bye riding, perhaps, on the outcome of this game, Zerck was taking dumb chances on the bases again. In the second inning he was unsuccessful in stretching a single into a double, but he pulled off a crazy, one-error inside-the-park home run in the fourth that energized us into three more runs after that.

But it was odd energy, considering the team was divided. Alex made sure of that.

I have always thought that everything everywhere was funny and though I knew that was wrong, I found that this was a great way to keep a lot of friends or at least long-term shallow acquaintances. Alex is something like that. He is a person who straddles the border between corrupt and correct. Although I can see why others may not like him, I simply think that Alex is Alex. He cracks me up and I've known him forever, so that's all that needs explaining.

When he showed up at the game and said, "Everybody, let's pull together now, then when the game is over we can argue," I laughed.

Then he said, "I won't point out now that James and Cindy and Gerald are wrong about Mission," and acted like he actually thought that would get us to pull together. When we actually did pull together, he seemed more surprised than the rest of us. There was a kind of tense energy as if the good electrons and bad electrons were bouncing off of each of us according to some complex algorithm that made us play almost angry.

Zerck came to the bench after his home run and we all high-fived him—some with enthusiasm and some by protocol.   .

"How's that for showing who is right about Mission?" said Zerck.

"A home run don't mean nothing," said Alex.

"Let's see you do it" replied Zerck.

"Let's talk about Mission," said Alex.

I was standing watching with my mouth open, thinking here we go again. I couldn't believe it. I'd seen it a million times on this team—two old friends staring each other down. Like Charlie, I'd done it a couple of times—with Zerck and with Bobby and with Alex, and with pretty much everyone else.

But this was different. This was about Mission.

"All right," said Zerck. "Let's talk."

Just then, Lisa lined the ball to left field and turned the corner at first base before backtracking when the hurried throw came in to second base. It was smart aggressive base running, forcing a throw and hoping for a mistake.

"I don't understand you, Zerck. But I don't care. Listen. Just because you and Cindy joined the forces of evil..."

"Peter Junkin?"

"Yeah, that's right. The forces of evil. Just because you and Cindy joined with the forces of greed and evil doesn't mean that this is a slam dunk," said Alex.

"Almost everyone except Victoria Manchester is in favor of this, Alex." Zerck stared hard at Alex. His voice lowered, "This is a real minor league baseball stadium," adding firmly, "that everyone in this town who counts is in favor of, and you know it."

"We're not," said Charlie.

Dawn grounded the ball to the third baseman who threw Lisa out at second. But the second baseman threw the ball over the first baseman's head and Dawn's double play turned into a double. There was one out and we were winning 3-2.

"What do you mean?" asked Zerck.

"We're against the project," I said to him. There it was. I was involved now. And for effect, I added, "People like us are against this. And we count."

"It's true," said Lisa, with a quick look over to me. She raised her chin to Zerck. "This is our baseball field. I don't care what kind of deal you cut, this is our baseball field."

"What are you talking about, deal? I didn't cut a deal," Zerck smiled. "It's just that, if you think about it, and I have, this is a particularly good idea for this town. Sure, it took me a while to figure it out, but I think you will too. Maybe not 'til it's built. But you will." He paused. "It's really gonna be amazing."

"It's not going to be built," said Alex.

"Who's going to stop it?" asked Cindy. She was on deck, taking her warm-up swings.

"We are," said Alex. "We're going to become political activists."

She stopped for a moment and looked at him.

"What do you know about politics?" She turned, and swung really hard.

"Nothing," I said. And when I said it, it brought an involuntary smile to my face. So I added, "Nothing at all."

After fouling off four pitches down the left field line, Corey turned the other direction and sent a ball tickling the foul line in deep right field. At the marsh, the outfielder picked it up. By the time the ball was in the infield, Corey was at third and Dawn had scored.

"That's why we're doing it," said Bobby. "If we knew anything about it, we wouldn't, see?" Bobby, as I've said before, is brilliant— like Aristotle.

Zerck and Gould took a step towards Bobby. They said nothing but their expressions said, *Bobby?* After all, he was the one who started the whole thing. Why would he work against it? Bobby acted oblivious to their confusion. He smiled at them. He walked to the bats because he was on deck.

Gould said, "So how are you going to do it?"

"We don't know yet," said Alex, "but we're having a meeting after the game for anyone who wants to help. And James, you can come too, if, you know, you want to spy."

"I don't need to spy," said Gould. "You guys won't be able to do anything. This is a guaranteed win. Where you are standing now is probably going to be a great place to buy a TV. A top-notch TV, if you can afford it."   .

Cindy hit a ball to the shortstop and he bobbled it, allowing Corey to score, and Cindy to be safe at first.

"But it doesn't matter what store is going to be here," said Gould. "The fact is that there *is* going to be a big beautiful mall here that almost all of Vermouth wants, and if you don't, fine. You're still gonna get it. And then, you'll like it."

Charlie hit a shot between the third baseman and the shortstop, and Cindy jogged into second. Bobby then hit a drive over the short fielder's head. When the right fielder came up with it, he threw to second, holding Bobby at first. But Corey was at third and Cindy scored making it 6-2.

With runners on first and third, I approached the plate with half a mind on this conversation, and I only have half a mind to spare. This spelled trouble. I always tried to have a business-like approach up there, even when I am laughing or angry. Like now. Now, I was intrigued, confused, angry, and, in a way, laughing. I had half a mind to say something.

"C'mon, Cletis," shouted Bobby from first base. He clapped his hands together. "Knock me in."

Behind me, I heard Alex say, "We'll see about that."

And then Gould said, "It's going to happen. And you're going to love it. I just know."

I swung as hard as I could. An angry swing. My arms, wrists, hips, and legs exploded onto the ball. For a brief instant I was sure I got all of it, but then I saw that I didn't.

As the left fielder easily tracked down my ball, I heard Zems, who had watched all the proceedings quietly, yell, "All right! That's the kind of inning I like."

After the win, we, *the Revolutionaries,* planned to gather on the mound. It was Alex's idea. Symbolic, he said. Good karma. It will feed our ideas, he said.

It was 5 p.m. The others—indifferent or against us—wandered towards their cars laughing, I'm sure, at the Quixotic nature of our meeting.

"Stopping a millionaire from making more millions is a noble cause," said Dawn, showing an understanding that belied her job at the bank, "but you can't do it."

Corey told us this was like "cutting off your noses to spite your faces." Which was not true at all. We all had our noses. I watched as Cindy walked off the field without even a glance at us.

You Can't Sell Right Field

But Zerck stuck around long enough to say, "You know, politics is only a game. You don't have to take it seriously. Especially not small town stuff like this."

Quiet.

"Look, I know you mean well. But c'mon, we've been friends forever. Let's keep it that way, okay?"

Silence.

"Jesus, guys. I had to do this. I had to." He paused. "The baseball stadium," he paused again. "You guys are crazy."

We stared.

Charlie said, "Gerald, just go away."

And he did, he walked from us into a different world, or at least different mode than us. He walked to Cindy who was standing by her car laughing with James Gould.

We walked the other way, to the mound and sat down. Alex, not surprisingly, brought a bottle of tequila, which he said, was the proper thing to fuel a revolution.

"Before we start," he said, "we should each take a shot to symbolize our unity."

Ah yes. More symbolism. This was turning into a symbolic revolt with no apparent substance other than the actual substances fueling the revolution. From the outside, from the likes of Zerck, it could not have looked like a promising start, symbolically drinking tequila on the pitcher's mound. But we were serious. At least I was.

So, without shot glasses, we passed the bottle around and found that a shot is an arbitrary thing. Charlie, for instance, took a couple of big gulps followed by a rasping *ya! ya! ya!* emanating from deep in his gut, an urgent plea against his brain to stop this poisonous invasion.

Then, just as the growl stopped, he shook his jowls twice and said, "Man, that's good."

Lisa, on the other hand, lightly tipped the bottle so that maybe she smelled it, maybe she tasted it, but neither was enough for her to do anything other than make a slight bitter face before passing the bottle to me, whereby I took, I'm sure, exactly a jigger's worth, swished the bitter liquid around my mouth, then let the fire drip down into my gullet. My eyes watered. The revolution was on.

"The first thing," said Alex, as we all sat down around the mound, "is that we have to be ready to take action as soon as possible. We all know that most people around here don't care about us, our softball field or anything other than the big bucks that Peter Junkin is promising to bring to town."

Around the circle it went and all of us—Bobby, Charlie, Lisa and myself—agreed to be ready. Ready for what? Who knew? But this is what we said.

"I'm ready," said Bobby.

"I'm ready," said Lisa.

"I'm ready," said Charlie.

"Yep," I said.

"So," said Alex. "Who has any ideas?"

For about 30 seconds, we sat quietly. Charlie cleared his throat. Lisa and I exchanged glances. Bobby scratched his head.

Finally Alex said, pleadingly, "C'mon. We said we were going to come here with ideas."

"All right," said Charlie. "How about if we hire one of those airplanes with a banner and we could fly it by all the beaches. You know, it could say, "Question 1 Ruins The Fun."

"You paying for it?" asked Alex.

"Well no, but..."

"We have a budget of zero," said Alex.

"That's not a lot," I offered.

"No, and it probably doesn't scare Peter Junkin too much."

"Think he'll find out about us?" I asked.

"He already knows, I'm sure," said Alex. "Don't you think Gould called him as soon as he left the game?"

"Or Zerck," said Bobby.

"Or Cindy, I guess," I said.

"So," said Alex, "they know that we are going to do something. But they don't know what and, it's funny, but neither do we."

"Two weeks," said Lisa. "That's all we've got."

"I think we should stand outside post offices with signs," I said. "You know, like Cindy does when she runs. Just standing there greeting people."

"Hey," said Alex, "that's a good idea. But then what do we say?"

"How about if we approach the *Messenger* and ask them to do a story about us," said Charlie.

"Yeah," I said, "we could get Zerck to go back to being a reporter and write the story."

This brought laughter.

"No, wait! Wait! Wait!" shouted Alex. "The *Messenger*! That's a great idea. They own this town."

"No, we own this town," I said. I was beginning to feel bold. Must have just been the tequila, For about the first time in my life I felt a sense of, I don't know, almost entitlement to my own opinion. I knew I didn't deserve much, being just a garbage man and all. But I was entitled, I thought as I sat on the pitcher's mound, to play softball on my favorite field in the world.

"That's funny, Cletis," said Alex. "We own this town? I like that."

"What's so funny?"

"Look at us," said Bobby. "None of us owns anything."

"Wait a minute!" said Alex. "I own a house."

"So do I," said Lisa.

"I've got a killer stereo," said Charlie.

"Yeah, and I own," I hesitated as I wracked my brain, "that piece of shit car over there."

"We don't own nothing," said Bobby, "nothing of value to match against Peter Junkin. What we own is symbolic."

Brian Tarcy

More symbolism. I had enough.

"I'm sick of it!" I said. "Symbolism! Fuck symbolism! Let's do something."

"That's the idea, Cletis," said Alex.

I don't know why but I suddenly tequila-realized that this was all some sort of reality—a place I did not want to deal with and it was making me crazy, claustrophobic even.

"We have to do something. They can't just do this to us."

And then a big white Frisbee flew into the middle of our circle.

"Hey chuckleheads!" came a voice from the east side of the field. "You look like a bunch of campfire girls."

"Lucky shot Ed," said Charlie to the approaching Ed Zems.

"You're the ones who just got lucky," said Zems, "because it just so happens that I'm pissed enough to want to help."

"You walked here?" I questioned. He hardly walked anywhere.

"Yeah. That's how pissed I am at this whole fucking thing. You guys are right. I never thought I'd say that. So I walked here. I needed to let some energy out." He sat down. "Hey, give me that bottle," said Zems, breathing heavy. He took a big snort and some dribbled onto his purple and white shirt. "Ahh."

Alex smiled at Zems like he was a big brother. "So what do you aim to do Ed?"

"Well, tomorrow morning I've got to drive Christine to the airport. She's going to the Bahamas, thank God. Then, I'm going to, I don't know." He shifted gears. "How does a thousand dollars sound? Does that help?"

"That's exactly one thousand more than we have," I said.

16

TASTES LIKE CHICKEN

The strangest day of my garbage career was surely the first because nothing can be more shocking to an aspiring non-garbage man than finding you are working inside of a garbage truck. But the second strangest day of my garbage career was August 22nd when Fred Glass offered me a chicken salad sandwich and then, after I took four bites and agreed that it was the best I ever tasted, he told me what was in it.

Red Cranial Woodpecker.

"I've been hunting," he said with a big dumb smile on his big round face. "I go early in the morning. Stupid birds just sit there waiting for me to shoot them."

"Are you crazy, Fred!"

"What? I thought you hated the bird. All you ever do is complain about it, complain you are losing your oh-so-sacred baseball field. Cletis, all you ever do is complain anymore. I thought you'd be happy

The truth is, even though there isn't much meat on them—hell there's five birds in each of these sandwiches—they do taste like chicken. Better, even!"

Now I am mostly a law-abiding citizen. Though small infractions like Alex's many idiosyncrasies don't bother me in the least, I thought that the moral line had been crossed by Fred and his hunting ways. Sure, I hated the damn bird, but that didn't mean I wanted Fred to hunt an endangered species. I believed that the whole endangered species thing was a good idea. And even though I still couldn't believe that this lost tribe up here in Vermouth were endangered, it still didn't seem right, shooting at little birds that took five to make a sandwich.

"Fred," I said. Then I couldn't even fathom a way to respond. It seemed Fred, who still hadn't gotten laid and reminded me from time to time, was trying to get on my good side. After all, it seemed, I was the professional and he, as he often said, was my apprentice.

"What?" he asked.

"Well, you know. This shooting of birds. It's not good."

"Why not?"

"Well, it's not helpful."

"If I kill all of them it will be. Won't it?"

When I got home that night, I called Alex and told him about Fred.

"If he gets caught, he better not tell anybody he got the idea from you," said Alex when he was done laughing.

"It wasn't my idea!"

"Sure, sure."

"It wasn't! I was shocked, I swear. Who would go out hunting for an endangered species? Especially by Mission Pond. It's bizarre. But I've told you about this joker before."

"So how many birds in a sandwich?"

"Five."

"How many sandwiches did he have?"

"Three. He ate two."

"So that's fifteen birds," said mathematical Alex. "Man, how does he fire off 15 shots over there and not get caught? I mean, he must have missed some too. How the hell?"

"He told me he used a silencer," I said.

Brian Tarcy

17

DIVIDED WE STAND

In the Wild Bird, I maintained that I was misquoted.

This is the quote attributed to me that appeared in the first paragraph of a front-page story in the August 25th *Messenger*: "I am not happy about the planned development on our baseball field. This doesn't seem fair."

What I actually said was, "Fuck Peter Junkiin. He's a greedy asshole."

My photograph appeared under the headline, "Garbage Man & Others Fight Mission." We had asked and gotten interviewed by a cub reporter, and somehow I became the loquacious one that the reporter connected with, so, despite my continued intention to remain anonymous and below everyone's radar forever I found that I was instead, a headline.

A fat photographer with a bad limp took my picture next to my garbage truck. When the paper came out people seemed to recognize me with odd, quizzical looks. Only one person, the heroin addict who sold me my powdered donuts in the morning, ever said anything about the article and that was, "I never knew you was a garbage man. I always thought you was a cop." She thinks everyone is a cop.

As we headed into the summit meeting that night, I, by virtue of the story in the paper, thought of myself as one-time spokesman for the baseball defenders among us. My counterpart on the environmentalist side was Victoria Manchester. Together, we were forming our own coalition of the willing—willing to fight Junkin.

Two concessions were made, one by each side of this meeting. First, Victoria Manchester and her friends agreed to allow the meeting to take place in the Wild Bird. Second, we agreed to let Victoria Manchester chair our committee, which we were calling, "Citizens Against Vermouth's Extinction"—CAVE was the acronym. It was dumb but no one had anything better and it was decided we needed a name so we could be identified in the *Messenger*.

"Could we *please* get the music shut off *please*," said Victoria Manchester in a loud prim voice, emphasizing each "please" with an eerie schoolmarm tone. *Whipping Post,* of all things, was on the stereo. Corey, who happened to be the manager that night, turned it off.

I couldn't quite figure Corey. He had no real interest in Mission but in conversations he generally supported the concept because of its potential impact on the Bird. Yet he encouraged us to have this meeting in his bar. Maybe he was just interested in getting dollars wherever he could—like everyone else in the world.

It started well. Two groups with no common interests united behind one cause, to stop Mission from completely changing the town of Vermouth. If anything, that sense of place—as different as each perspective was—was the cause. Birds or baseball, bongos or beer, it didn't matter what our sense of the place was.

The environmentalist didn't care a bit about our baseball field and we didn't give a damn about their bird. In fact, the two groups didn't much like each other. That was clear from dropped comments in the middle of sentences. We talked about the good done "by that stupid bird," and they talked about sentimental power of "your goofy baseball field." Divided we stood.

"Now," said Victoria, "let's look at what has happened so far. From our end, we've run an advertisement in the Messenger about the need to protect a much larger area for the Red Cranial Woodpecker than Peter Junkin is offering."

This made me laugh to myself, thinking of Zerck selling her an ad. It probably wasn't Zerck, but I hoped it was.

"We're planning to fly a banner by all the beaches on Labor Day Weekend saying, 'Question 1 Ruins The Fun,'" said Charlie proudly.

"I've gone to post offices and talked to people," said Bobby. "Sometimes I go in the morning, sometimes in the afternoon. It depends how tired I am when I get off work. But sometimes people even listen to me." He smiled.

"Well, we've challenged Peter Junkin to another debate," said Victoria. "We haven't heard anything back."

I said, "He seemed happy enough with the coverage he received in the Messenger the last time. He's probably ignoring us."

"He must be worried some," said Alex, "considering all the blue and orange all over town just since word of this meeting got out."

It sounded, to the cynical part of my ears to be let's-at-least-try sound effects. There wasn't a whole lot of passion in the room and then I stepped in with the lamest of all offerings.

"I bet they are plenty worried," I said. "I've begun to hear bits and pieces out there. You know, in stores, on my route, wherever. People actually recognize me and say now that they think about it maybe Mission isn't such a good idea." This wasn't exactly true. Only the heroin addict had even commented on the story and all it did was help her to realize that she had mistakenly connected my donuts to another career.

"Okay," said Victoria. "We can all feel that we are making some sort of tangible progress. But time is of the essence. September 5th is coming at us like a freight train."

And suddenly the date jumped at me.

September 5th really was coming at us like a freight train. I, like all of us, was tied to the train tracks. It seemed we were all congratulating ourselves. Not because we could stop it, but because we had the courage to say we really didn't want to get hit.

I took a deep breath. And from somewhere way deep where I have always wanted to let out that yowl, that speech at the Lincoln memorial, that one wild guitar riff, that scream from deep into a Tuesday afternoon in my childhood when it all just *hurt*, I smelled honeysuckle.

"No," I said suddenly. "They can't do this."

Everyone looked at me.

I stood, because again I wanted attention. What was I doing?

"No," I said louder. "They can't do this to us. They can not!"

I was frightened.

And then I smelled it again.

"Best as I know," I said before I even knew I was talking again, "this is my last pass through this town," adding, "and this country and this planet."

What the fuck was I talking about?

It was honeysuckle.

"It's not enough to try. We've got to do something. Something dramatic. We have to win."

"What is your idea, Clyde?" asked Victoria.

"My name is Cletis," I said, "and my idea is to do the most obvious of all the things we could. Let's tell the town the truth."

The truth was we didn't have much money. Zems stepped forward and took credit for all we that had and offered to do more if we could come up with a reasonable plan.

"I've been lobbying everyone in the Chamber and believe me,

folks, it ain't easy. These people only think about money," he said without any sense of irony.

Victoria then made baseball into afterthought. She had determined that the bird was our only real weapon in the argument.

"I got the whole project moved, didn't I?" she asked rhetorically.

As much as I wanted to respond, I was exhausted. I shrugged.

Then, with a bang the door to the bar flew open and in walked two men and two women wearing blue and orange outfits.

Our telegram, for your dear pumpkins
Comes from your friend, Peter Junkin
They sang...
You can try and try to cause a division
But it won't stop our plan for Mission
They tap-danced too...
So have your meeting and speak your words
And worry 'bout your endangered bird
But all is fine, if you catch our drift
And you'll find out on September fifth
Then they left.

It happened in under a minute.

And it sent our entire meeting into a parallel universe of mouth-dropping anger. We hadn't been spied on. We'd been invaded. Trolled. And the parallel universe, with the tackiest of invaders, was now the same as ours.

Anger has power. Say what you will about the power of love, but when it's from deep in the gut, anger is loaded with gunpowder. Zems, especially, was angry.

I was angry and so were Bobby, Alex, Charlie and, yes, Lisa too.

On the other hand, Zems was a businessman.

My anger at a base level was simple. I was mad because I couldn't keep doing something I'd been doing since I was eight and that was enough of a reason for me to change my whole outlook on things like my town and politics and even friends, such as Zerck. The rest of the group's anger was founded in much the same nostalgic place.

But Zems didn't have a nostalgic twinge about anything in Vermouth, and maybe not anything—not even his baseball career. Even his baseball career was not some great period from his life that he looked back at with rose-colored glasses. Instead, it was collateral—something to brag about, just like his businesses and his money and his large absurd house. No, Zems was angry about something more immediate than our concerns about the field of our youth. He saw those singers walk out the door after singing their taunting song, and he exploded in the most controlled way I had ever seen. He was famous among us for his many colorful outbursts.

This time he simply said, "That son of a bitch is making fun of us."

After Bobby left for work and the meeting was near breaking up, Victoria Manchester raised another issue that sent a little shiver down my spine.

"Finally, on a different subject, I don't know if anyone knows anything but I am simply asking you to keep your eyes and ears open," she began. "It has come to our attention that someone," and she paused, "Someone is, I think, hunting Red Cranial Woodpeckers at Mission Pond. Shells have been found. Nests are empty."

"I know nothing," I offered quickly. Maybe too quickly.

The others agreed that they also knew nothing. In truth, however, all my friends knew about Fred.

Zems gave us another thousand dollars to do with as we pleased.

"Leave the radio and newspapers to me," he said. "Peter Junkin is not the only person with money around here," he said.

Afterward, Lisa and I went back to her house and watched SportsCenter. During every local commercial break on the local cable, there were advertisements for Mission.

Peter Junkin, in a blue shirt with an orange collar, kept smiling into the camera from the shore of Mission Pond.

"Hello, my name is Peter Junkin and I am planning the greatest thing that will ever happen to Vermouth. I am the man behind Mission."

He smiled, and then a quick four-second graphic of the Mission blue and orange logo appeared.

"I'd like to assure you that my plan to change the town of Vermouth forever with the greatest development to ever come here is going to make you very happy. Please don't listen to those who say otherwise. We are saving the habitat for the Red Cranial Woodpecker. And soon we will have a great minor league baseball stadium. Please don't listen to scare tactics. Take charge of your future. Approve Mission, the greatest thing to ever happen to Vermouth."

He smiled sincerely. And on the screen came a blue and orange slogan, "Vote Yes On 1 For Profit And Fun."

"Ah ha!" I said to Lisa. "He did have spies. He knows our slogan. He ripped it off."

"Cletis, paranoia isn't good for you," she said.

"Did Peter Junkin program you to say that?"

18

I HATE MY BRAIN!

"It's gotten good, hasn't it?" Lisa said to me as she leaned across the bed over my naked chest. I reveled in my selfishness. This was good, yes.

"Us?" I asked.

She grabbed both sides of my face. "What do you think I'm talking about?"

"I guess, I don't know," I said, stumbling for the right answer.

Wrong answer. I knew when she pulled away, but by then my words were floating around the room like a lost bird.

"Cletis," she said. "What are you thinking about?"

"What do you think I'm thinking about?"

"I asked first."

I smiled.

"Not us, I guess. I don't know. You know, all the stuff."

"Thanks, Mr. Descriptive."

"Oh, this whole Mission thing has gotten to me, Lisa. I never expected anything like this. Frankly, I'm sick of thinking about it. I hate my brain! I just want it all to go away so I can do other things, like concentrate on us. Or nothing."

Concentrating on nothing seemed, right then, to be a noble goal. Wanting a vague, satisfying emptiness felt, though selfish, utterly honest. I stared into the deep pools that were Lisa's eyes. And I dove in. That's how good honesty felt. She smiled.

"I know, Cletis," she said. "Me too, you know. This is crazy. I never in my wildest imagination, I mean, yesterday, who would have thought I could have spent a day like yesterday, holding a sign and begging every person with a piece of mail to listen to my tale of woe."

"You spin a mean yarn," I said.

She kissed me. We parted and I took a deep, almost meditative breath. I felt it cleanse me, inside and out and as I stared back into Lisa's deep brown eyes, I had an epiphany.

"Yeah, I have to say that I have a lot more respect for politicians like Cindy," I said. "Well, maybe not what Cindy's doing, but that she does anything. I guess I mean I respect the dedication of politicians to a cause more than I did before. I mean, this is not fun. But you know, I think it's good to go through the process, follow the rules."

"Do you think we'll win?" she asked bluntly.

I hadn't even considered it for a while. Win?

"I don't know. I'd like to think so. You know. I'd like to think that between Victoria's bird and our baseball field, we could find the support in this town to save things. But, as Charlie always says, money talks. And this town is, well, this town. Money definitely talks here."

The phone rang.

"I'll get it," said Lisa, as she scampered to the other side of the bed to pick up the receiver. My still-astonished eyes went to the usual places on her naked body and when they did I had to admit that time had indeed made things better. It was comfortable. Funny about that word, comfortable. When I was young I thought comfortable was dangerous. Now, I yearned for nothing but. My fear of comfort had been transformed into the pain I felt without it. That alone made me feel really old.

"Hello," she said. "Uh, yeah," she said with an odd hesitation. She turned. "For you," she said.

"Cletis, I need help," came the voice I instantly recognized. "They got me."

Fred.

"What do you mean?" I asked, hoping I didn't know what I was sure I knew.

"The birds," he said. "They got me on the birds."

"Who got you?"

"I've been arrested. I'm down at the police station. I need some help."

"What? How? Why did you call me? How did you find me here?"

It was Sunday, August 27th, 8 a.m.

"I used the phone book. I found Lisa. Please. I don't have anyone else. Cletis. Please."

I knew he didn't have anyone else. At least no one else nearby, and maybe no one at all who would care as much as me. And I really didn't care very much.

Fred had told me in the garbage truck that he was from "a shit town in Pennsylvania." He came here 10 years ago with the main goal of not being in that shit town in Pennsylvania. He then wandered from job to job looking for answers, I guess that meant he wasn't much different than me except that he wasn't from here. And now, somehow, I was his one phone call. If you don't care a lot but have something of a conscience, there is nothing worse than being some-one's one phone call.

"Um," I said just like a garbage partner should. Mental

machinations about all this hurt my brain.

Birds. He killed birds. He killed birds for me.

I looked at Lisa who gave me a perplexed "What?" look. Then I looked at the floor, the walls—trying to find an easy answer written somewhere, but like my mind, they were blank.

"All right," I said finally. "I'll be there as soon as I can."

At 10:30 a.m., after walking out of the police station past a crowd—including Victoria Manchester and Ronald Dir—Fred was in the back seat of my sputtering Chevy talking about his hunting expedition. Just after sunrise, he said he was suddenly surprised by a bevy of cops, natural resource officers, and crazy sandal-wearing folks with binoculars.

"A lot of those people we just saw," he said. "They were really mean to me," he said with absolute surprise. He honestly didn't understand why they were angry. And he thought I was his inspiration.

It cost Lisa's credit card $300 and an hour of our time dealing with paperwork to get Fred out of jail. He looked pale and shaken when we first saw him but by the time we were out of the parking lot of the police station he was leaning practically into the front seat bragging about his new pesto Woodpecker recipe.

"It's delicious," he said. "I've just got to get a few more birds."

A crowd gathered at Mission Field for our game, which was the second of the day. When we showed up, Gorman's Landscaping was destroying Really Real Estate, 31-11, which means they had scored 31. A message game to us, I guess. That wasn't even what was astonishing. Really surprising was that this crowd was bigger than I had ever seen at this field before. Many people who had never bothered to watch our games were there, I guess, out of curiosity as to what was so damn special about this softball field.

So, there we were, still with Fred, getting out of the Chevy when a dozen or so of Vermouth's leftists noticed him, and me. This was not an especially good way to endear myself to the new coalition. As Gorman's shook hands with Really Real Estate, the leftists, mostly balding, bearded men in Tevas and barefoot women with gray hair and no makeup, began walking towards us. They gave off a rag-tag aura and yet their approach had a weird military air to it—organized, deliberate, and goal-oriented.

Lisa shot me a look that echoed what went through my mind— why did we bring this joker *here*? The answer was that after bragging about his recipe, Fred went through roller coaster mood swings that frankly worried me and not only that but he pressured us. He kept repeating, "I can't be alone today. Please take me to your game."

We brought him to Lisa's house after jail, fed him a lunch of tuna salad and then set him out on Lisa's back deck to sit alone while we gathered our baseball equipment together.

Fred sat in one of Lisa's white plastic deck chairs while we both rushed this way and that about the house. And he rocked, as if in a rocking chair. And he hummed, almost like a moan but there was a musical quality to his "mmm mmm" noises. His hands were folded on his lap and he just stared out at the trees.

At one point as Lisa was going this way and I was going that way she pointed at Fred, and I shrugged my shoulders. I didn't know what to say but I did know not to say that there were times in my life when I felt like doing exactly the same thing, just rocking away my blues. They were, of course, the most dangerous times of my life.

And now, on the baseball field, a dozen or so of the granola type approached us. On first glance, they seemed to be a different sort, same breed as Victoria Manchester and Ronald Dir, but more of a Ghandi-esque genetic code. An older, beautiful woman in a white sundress said, "Give peace a chance." She smiled at the bailed-out prisoner and at us, his protectors.

A different part of the species, a tattooed buzz-cut young man wearing a tie-dyed T-shirt with a peace sign on it bull-charged out of the group into Fred and sent him smashing to the ground. Just before he hit Fred, the man yelled out, "Bird killer!"

A loud noise went up from Fred. There was a thud. Around us, people gasped and then folks sitting in the stands, all the people leaving the Gorman's game and all those arriving for ours turned to see the angry young peacenik beating the shit out of Fred until I pulled him off.

"That's him," I heard from the crowd. "That's the garbage man."

On one side of the bench were:

Gerald Zerck

Cindy Morris

James Gould

Dawn Williams

Corey Everest

On the other side were:

Myself, Cletis Bord

Lisa Burton

Bobby Linster

Charlie Alderdi

Alex August

There was a space between the two groups and our body language, turned in different directions, clearly indicated that we were two different organizations with different agendas somehow working together towards the same goal—almost how Republicans and Democrats all claim with straight faces to be American first. We were Townies first.

"Team meeting," said Zems.

In all our years of playing together under Ed Zems he never called a team meeting just before a game. Usually, we got all our business taken care of during our once-a-week practice or else during a Zems' temper tantrum or, more likely, at the Wild Bird. It was a simple, bureaucratic system that had worked for years.

We all turned towards the front of the bench. Off of my side of the bench, on the ground with an ice pack over his swollen eye sat Fred, smiling dumbly and staring raptly at Zems. I could see in the way that he leaned forward that he felt like he was part of the team.

We looked out from our opposing sides of the bench. Zems stood. Charlie coughed. Zems stared at him. Quiet. I glanced up in the stands, and I saw Peter Junkin sipping coffee with the owner of Vermouth Concrete. Big game today, I thought. Lots of important people here. The quiet of our meeting went on for a minute, maybe a little more. Stares were exchanged back and forth. Zems looked at each one of us, one by one, right in the eyes.

Finally, he said, "Baseball is baseball. And the other stuff...is...the other stuff. This is baseball."

"It's actually softball," said Charlie.

About half of us giggled. I did. So did Bobby. And Zerck. Gould too.

Zems glared. And then another minute went by. More staring. I glanced over at Lisa who did not return my look. I scanned the stands again and saw my parents. ("I'm a voter," my dad would say later. It is all he would say to me so I said, "Good, vote against Question 1.") More stares. This was an odd Zems' tactic, this silence. But it was effective, slowing down our conflict enough so that we, as a team, would see that we, in fact, still existed as a team. The silence hung tensely until Zems seemed to sense our patience melting.

Zems turned to Corey. "All right, Corey you lead off," he said.

He spun and then turned back. "One more thing. This is a message game. We saw what Gorman's did. Let's let them know we can play too."

Then our two groups of five working in opposite directions some-how managed to destroy the group of ten working in the same direction that played for Vermouth Concrete. We won 18-1.

Throughout the game, though, we stayed on our own sides of the bench, talked each among our own groups and mostly talked about Mission in hushed conspiratorial tones. We had decided to work the crowd as soon as the game was over but by the fourth inning Charlie had begun walking the crowd, and soon we all did it.

"Please stop Mission," I said. "Don't let this beautiful baseball field disappear."

Some people, like the young family I first approached responded with a "You bet, we're with you."

An old woman sitting with an old man in plaid strapped carry chairs said, "I don't see what's so special about this. I'd rather watch real baseball."

The crowd seemed split down these two lines. After the game, as people walked to the parking lot we stood with a few members of the Vermouth Concrete team asking for support for the existing baseball field. "Please vote 'No' on Question 1," we pleaded.

When Zerck walked by with Cindy he had a scowl on his face. We had not talked as friends in two weeks. He was reduced to a mere baseball teammate and inflated into an actual civic enemy. He had a weird eye-averting way now. Looking at him, I could feel my face muscles tighten.

But Alex got him to look, and even smile, when Alex said, "Hey Zerck, I dare you to vote 'No' on Question 1."

19

BOBBY'S FLYER .

On new orders from Vic, Fred and I started work exactly when we punched in. No more coffee or chatting. When we pulled out of the parking lot from T&G Services, Fred drove while I cradled the remains of my chocolate milk. At my feet were only a *New Yorker* and a *People*. We drove about a mile down Superior Lane when I saw ahead, on the right, Bobby standing next to his car. He waved us down.

"Hey," I said, "That's Bobby. Pull over."

It was 7:15 a.m. Thursday, August 31st and we were headed to the old neighborhood, Sandy Hills, when Bobby flagged us down. As Fred slowed the truck to a stop I saw that Bobby was standing next to a brown cardboard box on the ground, and his car seemed full of similar boxes.

I got out of the truck. "What are you doing?" I asked.

He took a sip of his Gatorade.

"I got something for you," he said when I approached him.

"What are you talking about."

"I got some stuff printed up," he said.

"You got some what printed up?"

"Flyers. Stuff. I spent some of my Judas money," said Bobby. He sipped more Gatorade. "Look. You've got to give these to people.""But..."

"You've got Sandy Hills today, right?" he asked.

I nodded.

"Here's some tape too. Just tape these on their garbage cans."

"I can't do that," I emphasized. "I'll get fired."

Bobby smiled broadly. He looked at me, at the garbage truck, at Fred. Again at the truck, then back at me.

"You'll get fired?" he asked.

"Yeah, then what would I do?"

Bobby smiled again. "Play softball," he said.

What could I say? "Okay," I said. "I'll do it."

"I did it for you," said Fred for the thousandth time that week.

I was sick of the explanation, sick of talking about it but he kept bringing up his hunting arrest. There was always a first-thing-in-the-morning apology followed by a noontime recipe and late afternoon promise about a new strategy on how to get birds without getting caught.

Yesterday, I asked, "But when all the birds disappear, don't you think they're going to look in your refrigerator?"

"Cletis," he said, "you're funny. No, they're going to look in South Carolina."

He turned down Sunny Lane into the heart of Sandy Hills, where all the streets have happy names.

A quarter mile in he turned onto Fun Street where I climbed out with four flyers crumbled into one front pocket of my pants. I stuffed Scotch tape into the other. Quickly, I emptied three barrels at the first house. These post World War II clapboard houses, stuffed side-by-side on 1/8th -acre lots, lined up like obedient little soldiers offering their garbage to the toy truck driving down the road. This old neighborhood was my old neighborhood. It had a way of reducing my perspective of life to that of playtime. Yeah, the old neighborhood. This was once the entire world. I removed my gloves and began taping a flyer to a garbage can.

"C'mon!" yelled Fred. "We'll be here till 9 at this rate!"

He was right, but he was Fred. I had stereotyped him inside my brain where I could assume superiority. He was Fred, all right. Nobody was more Fred than he was, therefore, I thought, he had no right to say anything about anything. But he did anyway.

"Hurry up!" yelled Fred.

I quickly developed a better system that used far less Scotch tape and much more creative litter. And as I walked and emptied trashcans in my old bicycle stomping grounds, flyers paid for by Bobby's 'Judas money' fell into these cans, on the lids, on the ground, and into garages. When I saw Mrs. Yulian driving her silver Buick on Goodness Street, I flagged her down and handed her a flyer.

"Do you vote?" I asked her.

"Oh Cletis, good to see you," said Mrs. Yulian. She grabbed the flyer without looking at it. She had pink curlers in her hair. She was about 75. "How are your parents?" she asked. Mrs. Yulian lived exactly one block away from my parents for the last 50 years. She grabbed my arm, and stared with what I saw as her old gray eyes.

"Fine," I said. I was sure I knew about as much about my parents now as Mrs. Yulian knew. Pretty much nothing. I could have tried to expand and somehow engage Mrs. Yulian in a vague conversation about this obscure topic—her neighbors and my parents—but what would be the point? I had flyers to deliver. We were both in our own worlds, I guess. I guess all of us are, really.

As Fred turned the corner from Summer Lane to my old street, Perfect Road, he took the corner too wide and he had to shimmy the truck back and forth to squeeze it around the corner. It gave me a chance to stare at the road and therefore, another corner of my mind.

The first time I ever picked up the garbage in my old neighborhood, I was startled to find myself on these streets again. Startled and embarrassed. My parents told me they were embarrassed, so I was too. I think. But that was four years ago and now I can convince myself that I can work this neighborhood the same as any other, with utter disregard for any of its residents. Mostly I can.

Except when I remember. This is where we rode our bikes and played long hours of catch with a tattered baseball. I inevitably time travel when I work this neighborhood. It's usually not an entire memory, just a quick flash. I'll see the old Zerck garage, for instance, that I've seen a million times before and suddenly I'll remember a water balloon fight from when we were 12. This time as I passed the Zerck house, I didn't have time to catch a memory. Mrs. Zerck came out and grabbed her barrel—and her flyer. There she was, out the door at us and it wasn't even 8:30 yet.

Mrs. Zerck glanced at Fred. She examined her flyer. And she smiled at me, her white dentures gleaming while her eyes suggested... something... something completely different for Mrs. Zerck. Something I couldn't quite figure. Her expression fell, and she glanced at Fred one more time before turning, with her barrels and flyer in hand, back to her garage.

Then there I was. It's funny about my old house. On Thursdays when we come by here, for more than three years now, the curtains are all shut tight—a closed-off house. It wasn't like that when I first started, for the first few weeks. Then, the curtains closed. Since then, I've driven down this road on rare days off other than Thursdays and the curtains are always open. There's something about Thursdays, I guess.

This Thursday was no different and my parents' house was all closed off again. I barely paid it any mind as I methodically stuck another flyer between the lid and the can so that the 'residents' here—as I felt forced to think of them—would find it the next time they needed to use the trash barrel, hopefully before Tuesday.

Every week, this was so weird. But what could I do? That's what I thought. They were embarrassed that I was the town garbage man. So they didn't talk to me. Our relationship fundamentally changed when I became a garbage man. They think I failed. But the truth is, every Thursday, their cans are emptied.

When we reached Charlie's parents' house, Fred said he was sick of driving so we switched roles. His flyer strategy was different than mine. He just put it in the mailbox. At the next house he actually ran and stuck it in the screen door.

At the August house, I had a bitter flashback but it only lasted an instant. When we were teenagers, Alex's brother Arnold had a motorcycle accident that killed him. Arnie was the coolest person in the neighborhood. Now, the sight of the driveway suddenly brought me back to the day of the wake.

I walked down the street past many cars into a crowded living room where Alex said, "Cletis, dude. Arnie. Cletis."

I was folding my mind around this dumb old hurt when I saw Zerck, in Cindy's Suburban, pull up alongside our truck. From the passenger door emerged the fat photographer with a limp who got great shot of Fred handing him a brochure.

"Thanks," he said. "But I've already seen one."

Then a police cruiser pulled up behind Zerck. Then another one. The policemen approached Fred, who stood holding a trash can in one hand and a pile of flyers in the other. I climbed out of the truck. I stood next to Fred, and listened while two policeman asked if he was Fred Glass.

In the next half-hour I learned that Fred had been chased off of the land early that morning and that the police were going to arrest him that night. But Mrs. Zerck phoned her son about the flyer and Zerck told a reporter who sent a photographer and then called the police in order to prove that the anti-Mission people included a bird murderer who was now littering.

After Vic showed up and Fred was carted away in the back of the police car, Vic hopped in the truck with me and I reluctantly explained the box of flyers on the floor at his feet. When he told me not to give them out I thought about it and said I had to. He said if I did, I was fired.

So I hopped out of the truck with the flyers and began walking.

━━━━━━

(Bobby's Flyer)
QUESTION 1 RUINS THE FUN
Did you know?
Mission will:
Kill a bird
Ruin a walk
Destroy a great softball field
Use all the water
Bring too much traffic
Change the town for the bad forever
Really!
Paid for by C.A.V.E.

━━━━━━

At 10 a.m. I was with Bobby walking Market Beach on this last day of August. It was still warm, sun-scorching actually. It had only rained once that summer that I could remember—the night of Gould's party. Like the weather, I was in a drought facing a crucial situation. I was jobless and my plan was to try to save my all-brown baseball field because now I would have plenty of time to play on it. It was, perhaps, a pointless plan, but I executed it with passion. We had just played the night before, beating Carson's Cars and advancing to the championship game.

I was with Bobby getting more flyers when he reminded me that the *Messenger* was going to write about me and my cause and my garbage partner in the next day's paper.

"I bet they use 'Bird Murderer' in the headline," Bobby said enthusiastically. He smiled. "The *Messenger* really wants Mission."

"How do you know?" I asked.

"Do you *read* their paper?"

"I've seen it."

"They want high rises *and* they want to save the Red Cranial Woodpecker. They want everything."

"So do I." I smiled.

"I'm telling you, it's the media. They are the power behind this," continued Bobby.

"You are so grassy knoll," I said.

"I certainly am," he said. "The world is governed from a grassy knoll in Dallas." When we reached the beach, he turned to the first person he saw, a large woman with short hair, and he asked, "Do you know that Question 1 ruins the fun?" He gave the startled woman a flyer.

I passed out these goofy flyers to sunbathers—every person I could find on every towel.

"Please vote no on 1," I said over and over.

Meanwhile, Bobby was in the water giving them to swimmers. The flyers were already floating in the water. He didn't care. "Have a flyer," he said to a man who was already collecting litter.

They were dumb flyers. They really were. Bobby designed these stupid sheets of colored paper that had gotten me fired. When I ran into him at the water's edge, I began talking about my lost job because I couldn't stop thinking about it.

"Cletis, you were a garbage man," Bobby said.

"I was a good garbage man."

20

BANKS LOVE SHYSTERS

I joined the revolution for lunch, since I was fired and had nothing better to do. I joined the group that gathered at the Wild Bird to discuss tactics and strategy but quickly heard, "What's he doing here."

The loud complaint came from a balding man with a ponytail who I immediately recognized as one of those who saw me bail out Fred.

When I explained how I thought I had been set up and that the other side was playing hardball politics, the same man from before said, "That's a sad story. Now get out of here. You're not part of us. You bailed out the bird murderer."

Bobby nudged me. It was the *Messenger* ad sales guy, Zerck, I explained, who was responsible for the whole incident on Perfect Road that morning. I took a breath and stopped. I didn't know what else to say.

We were days away from losing the greatest ball field on earth—being voted out of existence. It hurt. Losing a place felt almost like losing a person. It would be like losing love except that sometimes you can lose a terrible love and only find out later that losing it was the greatest thing that ever happened to you. Losing Mission Field could never feel that way.

"Bird murderer," said another man.

Then a young woman in hoop earrings and combat boots, "Bird murderer."

Fred had been projected onto me. As I felt the hate pierce me, Alex jumped to my defense and said I was on their side and that he believed it was time for us to play politics too.

"This is crazy! Let's fight back!" he shouted at the end.

"Already being done," chirped in Zems calmly, with a sly smile.

"What are you talking about?" asked Victoria. She also smiled, almost with admiration.

"You'll find out," he said. He smiled back at Victoria. And then he looked at Bobby, who looked at me, and I shrugged. But I was also not the topic of conversation any more and for that alone I was thankful. Still, ponytail man glared at me.

"Now, before we go on, if you will allow me one indulgence?" Zems asked Victoria. He didn't wait for her to smile or nod. He turned to us, "Championship on Sunday folks. Remember, when it's baseball, it's baseball."

"We know," said Alex.

"Okay," said Zems. He cleared his throat. He looked at the hairy environmentalists, "I think what happened to Cletis sucks. Toying with lives is not funny. Just so they can have their big roads and big buildings and drive their Mercedes around. It's wrong."

"What if they drove Chevys around?" I asked.

"Wouldn't matter," said Zems.

"What are you talking about?" asked Victoria again, this time a bit impatiently. "Time is running out." She smiled again at Zems.

"What time is it?" asked Ed.

"Twelve thirty," said Bobby.

"Well, he should have been here at 12. So just cool your jets." He smiled at Victoria.

"Who should have been here?" I asked.

Zems turned to the front door and smiled. Bobby pointed to the doorway of the Wild Bird. There, at the entrance, I saw Matthew Linster.

"Car dealer friend of mine," said Zems. "We've been talking for a few days and well..." He turned to the door.

We all knew Matthew. He was essentially part of the group back in the day.

"Sorry I'm late Ed," said Matthew in a voice that had the same Linster ring I was used to hearing from Bobby, "but it took longer than I thought. Traffic."

He turned to the rest of us. He looked at the Victoria Manchester side of the room and said, "For those of you that don't know me my name is Matthew Linster. And I guess, unwittingly, I started all of this." He looked at Bobby. He nodded. Bobby nodded back.

"The reason I am here is that I just got back from the offices of the Vermouth *Messenger*. You see, I had a story to tell and so I thought I would come here and share it with you as well."

"As many of you know, I was raised in Vermouth. And I love this town so I have always stayed in touch by subscribing to the *Messenger*. Well, when I started reading stories about my little brother and his efforts, along with all of you, to stop this Mission project I became interested. I mean, Bobby never gets worked up about anything," he said, garnering enough laughter to continue.

"So I thought this must be important," said Matthew, "and when my friend Ed called and told me that he was also involved, well, you know. I used to play on that field."

He then described his college years at Boston University and just when it seemed his tangent was leading nowhere he mentioned that his old college roommate happened to work for the Miami Herald. In talking to this roommate, Matthew mentioned the entire Mission project and when Matthew told his friend about Peter Junkin his friend said he'd never heard of him and he'd see what he could find out.

"That was how I came to find out the truth about Peter Junkin," said Matthew with a large smile.

A stir went up around the Bird and Matthew knew just how to play it. He waited.

Then he said, "Peter Junkin is a complete fraud. He was never in the military, let alone a fighter pilot. He is not related to Walt Disney, and he owns no Disney stock. His real name is Peter Jones, and he can't even ice skate."

"Where'd he get the money?" asked Zems.

"Banks," said Matthew. "Mostly one big Boston bank. They believed everything he said."

"So did most of this town," said Victoria, smiling almost lovingly at Zems now.

"But," said Bobby, looking at Matthew, "he paid us."

"Right. Like I said, he got his money from banks. They loved him, loved his story. He was an ice-cubes-to-Eskimos kind of guy, and banks love shysters."

"More than honest people?" I asked.

Matthew laughed, and then Zems did too.

21

EXTRA INNINGS

.

"We can't lose!" shouted Bobby from second base. We were in the 13th inning. It was the championship against Gorman's Landscaping. It was Sunday, September 3rd, the crowd was huge and Labor Day weekend boisterous. Despite or perhaps because of Friday's *Messenger* stories about Peter Junkin—"Junkin May Be Sunk"—and about myself as connected to Fred Glass—"Bird Murderer Had Career In Garbage"—there remained great interest in this ball field and especially in this particular game.

And after we had dramatically pushed it to a tie in the 13th inning, Bobby declared that we may not win but we surely couldn't lose. Scoring four runs right after they scored four runs in the top of the 13th is downright insane. It was 12-12. We could tie forever.

Zems paced.

We were still up. I was up.

Bobby clapped from second base. The first pitch was way outside and I let it pass. I looked over at the bench and I saw everyone up on their feet. In the stands, the crowd also was standing. Peter Junkin—or was it Jones now?—was there because he just didn't care. He wanted to be seen. He was denying the *Messenger* story and working to get Question 1 passed. Everyone was there. Elliot Burren the architect was sitting with Junkin and three days ago this would have been a really scary sign.

But now this was a good sign. Elliot Burren was symbolically the perfect hire for this stage of Junkin's journey. Since Junkin couldn't possibly have enough money to have his dreams come true, it was sport to look at Junkin and Burren and imagine what these two would scheme up. Still, the *Messenger* claimed Junkin was sunk. That's what I was thinking as I swung at the second pitch with everything I had. I smashed it way over third base.

Foul.

"C'mon Cletis!" yelled Bobby.

"Hit it fair!" shouted Zems.

The whole world was there. All of my dreams, in one pitch. I could make a difference. It was in my hands.

And then, the next pitch.

And... and... and I watched it. I watched as the most perfect pitch ever thrown floated by me in the slowest motion I've ever seen. It seemed to stop mid air, as if on a tee only better. It was pure. I could have crushed it. It was engineered, designed to go into my wheelhouse. I stared at it, astonished, dumbfounded—just dumb. But I couldn't think about it. For that pitch I was completely and disgracefully not in the moment. I was, instead, off on another mental tangent that had nothing to do with that perfect pitch. Instead, for the six or so seconds that the entire sequence took, from the time the pitcher indicated he was about to toss me the most beautiful pitch since cavemen swung clubs, to the moment the catcher caught the ball with a sarcastic "Good eye, Cletis," the baseball part of my brain was worried about the election.

Luckily, in this league no one called balls and strikes. But still, I played the fool.

The next pitch was way inside. It would have hit me. And then came the one I shouldn't have gone for—that's what I thought mid-swing. I was wrong, way wrong. I hit the ball over the second baseman's head into right center field. It was a shot and it rolled.

And rolled.

And rolled.

And I ran.

And Bobby ran.

And it rolled, and when Bobby scored I was almost to second base, jumping up and down like a maniac, waving my arms, shouting. The entire team jumped, enthralled, captivated by the moment. Gloves flew. Beer flowed. Zems was shouting, giving Bobby the biggest hug you've ever seen. Charlie stood with a blank look on his face, overwhelmed as I saw it. Alex bounced and bounced. Zerck and Cindy were dancing on home plate. Dawn was hugging Corey.

Gould ran to Bobby and Zems.

"Champions!" he shouted, raising both arms in the air.

"Here Cletis," said Charlie.

I looked at all my friends and I found that they made me feel like the luckiest person in history. All of it—the sunset falling over the yellow flowers in left field, and everything else somehow crushed their way home, into my heart.

I ignored the rest. I pretended I didn't know about the fraud of Peter Junkin, the betrayal of Gerald Zerck, the departure back to some shit town in Pennsylvania for Fred Glass. I just smiled like a champion.

We had been there a while, the whole team. Smiling, laughing. Talking only baseball.

And then as Lisa and I walked to my car, she kissed me.

"I love you, Cletis."

22

FREEDOM OF SPEECH

I kissed Lisa and headed to the polls in South Vermouth. Things were changing. I was taking action. We both knew how we would vote.

"I love you," she said. Three overwhelming words.

"I love you," I said back.

This love, when Lisa joined in, was fast and I was happy, proving again, even at my age, that love is good.

I drove to vote, thinking it all through.

I was sure Mission would be defeated. After all, Peter Junkin was arrested the day before. The morning *Messenger* had pictures of him in handcuffs for fraud— "Junkin's Dreams Fail, Now Jail."

But not all felt well, of course. While Zerck told us he got a big bonus at the paper, because he brought in so much advertising during the election, Cindy had to resign from the board of selectmen. It was fast, like losing my job. One domino after another. Summer had fallen all over us like rain and now the immediate future of our summer playground was being decided by September's voters. As I drove to the school, I considered that the whopping piece of land out by Mission Pond would surely change sometime. A group from the Chamber calling itself 'Vermouth For Mission' took out a full-page advertisement in the *Messenger* on the day of the election. The ad promoted the zoning change.

"Someone will want to develop this great land. Vote for the change," said the ad.

And as I pulled in to the school, there was a dozen or more people holding blue and orange signs that said, "Vermouth For Mission." I didn't know what to think.

Then, across from them I saw Victoria Manchester holding a sign against Mission. I flashed her a peace sign and she actually smiled at me.

Most likely it would be houses. Someone—Zems has already talked about it—will come in within a few years and change the land forever. But was it going to happen now? For once, I knew what I wanted.

I voted 'No'.

And then when I left the school while I was walking to my car, I felt a splat on my head—a perfectly aimed bird dropping.

23

POMPOUS CIRCUMSTANCE

On Wednesday, I drove my new used Chevy, recently purchased at Zems Chevrolet, from my new home, inside of Lisa's house, to my new job as a janitor at EZ Chevrolet. I felt revived—a born-again pagan. I had cleaned up my own reputation inside of my own mind.

My world changed, as if a giant development of experiences had rooted in a far corner of my brain and flashed orange and blue neon memories at me. I was stronger, more... more something. I'd found love. For this moment, it felt pure.

I think that for now Lisa and I seemed to have found something exactly like bliss. And that's weird—weirdly great, lustfully scrumptious, comfortably wonderful, honorably perfect and all those what-was-I-thinking things that I fear won't possibly be real in five years but feel incredibly fantastically real right now. So that counts for something.

And other things do too. Mission, as a sort of event, counts in my life, I know. On Wednesday, the vote was in. The battle was over.

On Wednesday, as I was driving home from EZ Chevrolet, I realized that I really did feel like a new human being. I liked my new job. Zems was sort of like Charlie was when I worked at the market all those years ago. Zems liked me. He told me I could move into the parts department within six months. So I had that dream.

After work, we sat in his large office full of portraits of Zems and he told me boastful stories about the year when he played in 27 games for a horrible New York Mets team. In one game, he got three hits, including a home run. It was the best day of his life.

On the drive home, I stopped at Market Beach for a moment and saw a cloud shaped like a garbage can. I finally understood. I took charge of my life. Being abandoned can make you do that. This whole thing made me feel that way. My town didn't care about me. But my friends did. Lisa did. I discovered I did too.

When it was over I realized on walking into Lisa's house—my home—that Wednesday after my first day on my new job that I'd just finished growing up. It made me a bit sad. It meant, I think, that I knew I wouldn't really ever change much. I'd always eat cheeseburgers, play softball on some field as long as I could, and work a menial job helping people who have more money than me. These were the stars I reached for.

Even though during all these years I thought I was just in a phase, I realized on Wednesday that I was really more in my permanent adult phase. And the melancholy of that realization that these were my adult activities meant I would most likely not travel the world or build a skyscraper.

But it meant something else. I smiled as I thought. I cherished the life I'd built, even with its flaws.

It had to do with all these people, these teammates, and this little town. It had to do with Lisa. And it had to do with me. I was happy.

Mostly, I was glad I finally had my say.

Ah, maybe I didn't grow as much as I think. I give myself way too much credit. But here's the truth. It was my vote, one vote anyway, that made the difference in the election.

That night at the Wild Bird, Bobby bought cheeseburgers and beer for everyone. The whole team was there.

THE END

ABOUT THE AUTHOR

Brian Tarcy is co-founder of Cape Cod Wave online magazine (CapeCodWave.com). He is a longtime journalist who has written for the Boston Globe, Boston magazine, the Cape Cod Times and several other publications. He is also the author or co-author of more than a dozen books, including books with celebrity athletes Cam Neely, Tom Glavine and Joe Theisman. His previous book was a non-fiction business thriller, *ALMOST: 12 Electric Months Chasing A Silicon Valley Dream* with Hap Klopp, who created the iconic brand, The North Face.

Made in the USA
San Bernardino, CA
25 May 2020

72299467R00095